Birding
in Central and Western
New York

Best Trails and Water Routes
for Finding Birds

by Norman E. Wolfe

Every effort has been made to provide accurate and up-to-date trail and waterway descriptions in this book. Hazards are noted where known. Users of this book are reminded that they alone are responsible for their own safety when on any outing and that they use the routes described in this book at their own risk.

If you find inaccurate information or substantially different conditions (after all, things do change), please send a note detailing your findings to:
Footprint Press, P.O. Box 645, Fishers, NY 14453
or e-mail: rich@footprintpress.com

The authors, publishers, and distributors of this book assume no responsibility for any injury, misadventure, or loss occurring from use of the information contained herein.

Birding
in Central and Western
New York

Best Trails and Water Routes
for Finding Birds

PO Box 645, Fishers, NY 14453
http://www.footprintpress.com

Other books available from Footprint Press:

Locations by Number

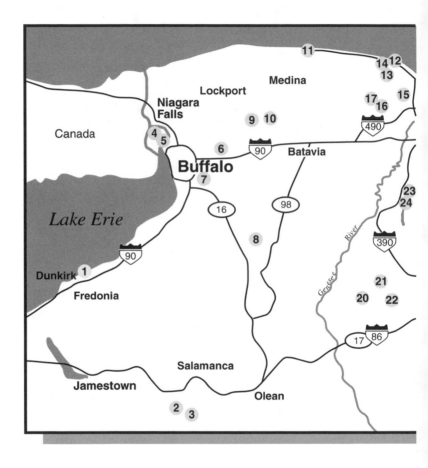

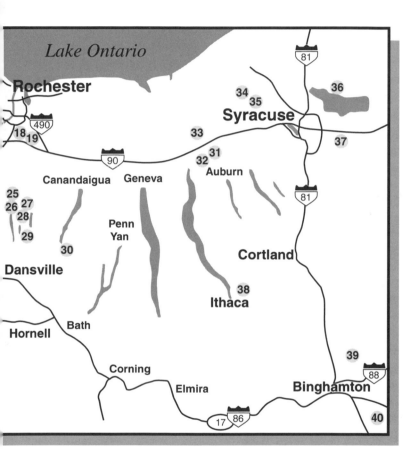

Lake Ontario

Rochester

490

18 19

90

Canandaigua   Geneva

25
26 27
28
29

30

Dansville

Penn
Yan

Bath

Hornell

Corning

Elmira

34 35

Syracuse

33

32 31

Auburn

36

37

81

81

Cortland

38

Ithaca

39

Binghamton

88

17 86

40

Contents

Acknowledgments

I wish to thank my English teacher Miss Ethyl Dunn at Rochester's John Marshall High School, who encouraged me to keep trying. Thanks to my friend Dick Groves who camped on the snow and canoed with me throughout the Northeast and Canada. Thanks to my friend Lois Asandrov who supplied support in starting this book and to Footprint Press for its patience. Many thanks to my relatives Jane, Sylvia and Elizabeth (Chickie). Thanks to Ken (Bluebird) Waters for his friendship. And, as his past scoutmaster, I extend my gratitude to Eagle Scout Jonathan Woodard for the artwork used in this book.

Many thanks go to my immediate family, including my son John, his wife Mary and grandchildren, Mike and Kathryn, for their help; my son Steve, his wife Kelly and grandchildren, Noah and Madalyn, for their encouragement. To my daughter Karen, or "Bunk," as I call her, thanks for showing me how to hang in there.

Most importantly, to my wife, Joanne Wolfe, I extend gratitude to the nth degree for all the love, help and support she's given me through the years:

I dedicate this book to her.

Then there are all the dedicated naturalists, rangers, birders, park managers, and others who assisted with this book. To each I extend a sincere thanks:

Kevin Brazill, Diane Wheelock, NYS OPRHP, Green Lakes State Park

Grace Christy and Daniel Davis, NYS OPRHP, Allegany State Park

James Eckler, Don Eddinger, Dan Carroll, Ron Schroeder and Bruce Penrod, NYS DEC, Avon

Daryl Jenks, Wesley Stiles, NYS DEC, Cortland

Ronald Abraham, NYS DEC, Belmont

Mark Kandel, Pat Nelson, NYS DEC, Buffalo

William Michalek, Buffalo Audubon Society, Beaver Meadow Audubon Center

Marie Petuh, Naturalists' Club of Broome County, Inc.

Ed Hart, Broome County Parks and Recreation

Greg Smith, Beaver Lake Nature Center

John Plummer, Town of Greece, Department of Highway, Sewer & Park Management

Thomas E. Tasber, Broome County, Department of Parks and Recreation

Donald Root, City of Rochester Water & Lighting Bureau

Eric Johnson, Eileen Kennedy, Russell Sciolino, Forrest Skelton, Monroe
  County Parks Department
Dorothy Gerhart, Iroquois National Wildlife Refuge
Daena D. Ford, Braddock Bay Raptor Research
Wayne Hale, Jr., County of Orleans, Department of Planning
  and Development
Marva Gingrich, Montezuma National Wildlife Refuge
Ed Fiorino, Lake Plains Waterfowl Association
Al Klonick, founder of *The Kingbird*
John Michaelski, Chenango Valley State Park
Tim Gallagher, Cornell Lab of Ornithology
Benjamin Morey, Buckhorn Island State Park

Preface

I noticed through years of teaching bird courses and seminars, that many students got excited when I mentioned alternative ways to enjoy nature and birding. They soaked up the basic knowledge of habitats, feeding, watching and identifying birds in the backyard; but every time I told them about birding explorations, they wanted to know more.

Although there are many books on birds and birding, there isn't much available on the *where to* and *how to* go birding. When my son Steve said, "You can reach more people with a book," it made sense to write a book about how to plan and execute an adventure based on my extensive experience. So, with the encouragement of friends, family and people who expressed the desire to learn, I wrote this book.

I also wrote it for people who may not know how to interact with birds and nature safely, or, to do it with minimal impact on our environment. Also, I hope to expose other outdoor people (hikers, bikers, hunters, etc.) to the enjoyment of birds so they can blend birdwatching with their activities for added enjoyment.

Believe it or not, I'm often asked, "Can you birdwatch from a canoe as well as while walking?" The answer is "yes." A canoe puts you in a riparian habitat where the majority of birds are found. Plus, with a lower profile and the ability to proceed silently in this habitat, you gain a definite advantage. Opportunities for birdwatching can come from a trail, bike, snowshoes, skis, kayak, canoe, and even a car.

Are you curious about *where to* and *how to* go birdwatching? Are you looking for an additional way to enjoy the outdoors and explore nature? Then welcome to *Birding in Central and Western New York - Best Trails and Water Routes for Finding Birds*.

Introduction

The routes in this book are intended to provide a sample of what's out there to enjoy. No doubt, there are other good areas. This book will give you a starting point and encourage you to continue exploring.

With each route, I mention what birds you're likely to see. But there's no guarantee that certain birds will be present when you go. Migration patterns, weather, time of year and many other factors affect which birds you'll see. For example, warblers may be common in the spring but rare in the summer. See page 24 for a chart that will help you be at the right place, at the right time to find birds.

The routes in this book are rated for difficulty from 1 to 3; with number 1 being easy and 3 being most difficult. I included mostly easy to moderate routes; appropriate for families. Some of the journeys can be expanded for the more experienced. A few of the canoe routes may be easy in the summer but can change to rapids or rough water in the spring and when a lot of rain has fallen. Some areas become difficult to paddle in the fall, when low water conditions prevail.

Predicting trail and route changes or conditions is impossible. And, admission fees, where charged, could change at any time. As an individual or leader of a group it is your responsibility to check on current conditions before heading out. Don't go beyond your ability or the ability of the group's weakest person. Start with the easiest routes and build to the more difficult ones as you gain experience. Keep in mind that level of difficulty will increase in adverse weather. Use common sense and prepare for any outing. Better yet, take what you need for at least one level colder or wetter than conditions at the start of the journey.

Times mentioned to complete the routes are general guidelines. If you take longer, it could mean you're enjoying nature and seeing many birds; and this, after all, is the objective. The focus should be on keeping safe and having fun with minimal impact to the environment. Plan to take your time.

Some areas do not allow pets. Check with the contact listed before taking your pet along. Also, if you want to boat, fish, hunt or camp, be sure to check beforehand and obtain any required licenses or permits.

Plants look more beautiful when left in their natural surroundings. Don't pick any vegetation. Besides, it could be endangered or poisonous.

If you're hiking or canoeing in areas with a lot of waterfowl, don't feed them. Bread is not a natural food. It's processed food and isn't good for them. If people food is readily available, it might lessen their natural urge to migrate. High waterfowl concentrations make big messes and more importantly, the birds become susceptible to disease. If they migrate they carry the diseases with them to infect other areas.

I tried to include routes with enough variety for everyone. This includes a few for the elderly or handicapped that can be done by car as well as by biking or walking. These are listed in the index on page 151.

The majority of routes are designed to be enjoyed in the spring, summer and fall, either on foot, by bicycle, or by hand-powered watercraft. Personally, I like the spring and fall because of the increased number of birds during migration. Winter offers the possibility of more sightings due to lack of foliage. By putting on your snowshoes or cross-country skis you can have year-round fun.

Legend

At the beginning of each trail or water route listing, you will find a description with the following information:

Location: The town and county where the trail or route is located.

Directions: How to find the trailhead or boat launch parking area from a major road or town.

Admission: The entrance fee (if any) to use the trails or waterways.

Trail or Route Length: How many miles of trails or waterways are available.

Time to Hike or Canoe: Estimated time it will take to follow this trail at a slow pace or leisurely paddle. Of course, stops to scout for birds can extend the time measurably.

Trail or Water Conditions: A description of the physical condition of the trail or body of water.

Trail Surface: The type of material which comprises the trail bed, such as grass, dirt, or rock.

Trail or Route Markings: Markings used to designate the trails in this book vary widely. Some trails are not marked at all but can be easily followed. Other trails are well marked with either signs, blazes, or markers, and sometimes a combination of all three. Blazing is done by the official group that maintains the trail.

Signs – wooden or metal signs with instructions in words or pictures.

Blazes – painted markings on trees showing where the trail goes. Many blazes are rectangular and placed at eye level. Colors may be used to denote different trails. If a tree has twin blazes beside one another, you should proceed cautiously because the trail either turns or another trail intersects.

Sometimes you'll see a section of trees with painted markings which aren't neat geometric shapes. These are probably boundary markers or trees marked for logging. Trail blazes are generally distinct geometric shapes and are placed at eye level.

Markers – small plastic or metal geometric shapes (square, round, triangular) nailed to trees at eye level to show where the trail goes. They also may be colored to denote different trails.

It is likely that at some point you will lose the blazes or markers while following a trail. The first thing to do is stop and look around. See if you can spot a blaze or marker by looking in all directions, including behind you. If not, backtrack until you see a blaze or marker, then proceed forward again, carefully following the markings.

Difficulty Level: 1—Easiest. Appropriate for small children and novices. Generally a flat trail or calm water.

2—Moderate. The trail may have a more uneven surface or hillier terrain. The waterway will be flowing, wavy, or shallow.

3—More Difficult. The trail is physically demanding. The waterway has some rapids or obstructions to be maneuvered around.

Note: Any of the trails or water routes can move up to the next level of difficulty during bad weather, seasonal changes, or significant rain.

Birds Likely Seen: The species of birds commonly seen at this location.

Other Park Uses: The other activities allowed or offered at this location but not necessarily on the route described.

Contact: The address and phone number of the organization to contact if you would like additional information or if you have questions not answered in this book.

Map Legend

Symbol	Description	Symbol	Description
‑ ‑ ‑ ‑ ‑ ‑ ‑ ‑	Main Trail or Canoe Route	★	Trail or Launch Location
‑ ‑ ‑ ‑ ‑ ‑ ‑ ‑	Other Trail	●	Water
▬▬▬▬	Major Road	■	Park Boundary
─────	Secondary Road	▦	Marsh
++++++++++++	Railroad	**P**	Parking
(canoe)	Canoe Launch & Parking	(104)	Route #
✈	Airport	(90)	Interstate Route #
■	Building	╳	Bridge
⑰	Trail Post Number		

Trail Blaze Colors:

Blue - Ⓑ	Orange - Ⓞ	White - Ⓦ
Brown - ⒝ⓡ	Purple - Ⓟ	Yellow - Ⓨ
Green - Ⓖ	Red - Ⓡ	
Grey - ⓖⓨ	Violet - Ⓥ	

Migration

Honk, Honk, Honk ... you hear it first and look up into the sky to see a V of Canada geese flying overhead. It may be spring or fall. The annual migration has begun.

Each spring birds head north—some to the northern reaches of Canada. In fall they reverse directions and head south to overwinter along the Atlantic coast from New Jersey to the northern part of Florida. Most congregate in the Chesapeake Bay region. Mid-way between these summer and winter nesting grounds lies Central and Western New York, part of the Atlantic Flyway.

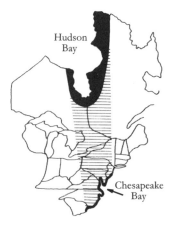

That's why in early April and again in October, we hear the honking and watch places like Iroquois National Wildlife Refuge, Beaver Lake Nature Center, and Tillman Road Wildlife Management Area fill with thousands of birds. Waterfowl like the Canada geese rest on the ponds, lakes, and swamps and feed during the day on nearby grasslands and winter wheat sprouts in spring fields or left over grain crops from the fall harvest.

Geese, blackbirds, warblers, and others—their times may be different but their purpose is similar. Males often arrive first in spring to establish and defend good territory. Then the females come to choose their territory to rear their young. Territory limits breeding numbers and determines nesting success.

Canada geese* are our noisiest migrators but by far aren't the only ones. Robins*, hawks*, blackbirds, and swallows migrate during daylight hours. Wrens, vireos, woodpeckers*, and warblers migrate at night. Ducks, geese, loons, and shorebirds migrate day and night. Migratory distances vary from a few miles to 11,000 miles. Even bats and some butterflies migrate hundreds or even thousands of miles.

No one knows what originally caused birds to migrate. Theories abound including glacial surges, overcrowding in tropical areas, and others. Today, migration is a built-in behavior driven by internal and external stimuli. These include length of day, temperature, food availability, other birds, fat deposition, hormone secretions, and the biological urge to breed.

Regardless of the reason, migration creates a spectacle to behold. And, in Central and Western New York, we hold ring-side seats.

*not all of these birds migrate

Important Bird Area Program

The aim of the Important Bird Area (IBA) program is to identify sites in each state that are essential for sustaining naturally occurring populations of bird species, and to protect or manage these sites for the long-term conservation of birds, other wildlife, and their habitats.

The program started in Europe in the 1980s. The New York State IBA program was launched by the National Audubon Society in 1996. Currently 127 sites have been identified in New York State including the following which are described in this book:
- Dunkirk Harbor & Point Gratiot Park
- Allegany State Park
- Iroquois National Wildlife Refuge
- The Niagara River Corridor
- Braddock Bay
- Hemlock/Canadice Watershed
- Hi Tor Wildlife Management Area
- Northern Montezuma Wetlands Complex

The criteria for becoming an IBA include:
- supports an exceptional diversity of bird species
- contains habitat type that is rare, threatened, or unusual
- is an exceptional representative of natural or near-natural habitat
- supports long term research and/or monitoring

IBAs assure multiple habitats are available to support the annual cycle of birds. A great blue heron, for example, needs shallow water or wetlands for feeding and a nearby forest with large crowned trees for nesting. Migratory birds passing through the area, such as the common loon depend upon open water for resting and feeding. The red-headed woodpecker requires sixteen to twenty snags per acre whereas the pileated woodpecker requires only one snag but many acres of land. Large areas of contiguous forest and water are important to the bald eagle.

Additional information on the Important Bird Area program is available on web sites:

http://ny.audubon.org/iba/what.html
http://www.audubon.org/bird/iba

What Are Birds?

A bit of bird history and knowledge of their remarkable biology will help you enjoy your birding adventures. The evolutionary changes that took place, and continue to take place, are intriguing and provide insight into how remarkable birds truly are.

Adaptation and Evolution of Birds

Scientists classify birds as Aves, and they are often referred to as feathered bipeds, meaning two-footed animals with feathers. Birds are warm-blooded, inner-skeletal, oviparous vertebrates (egg laying vertebrates). Through evolution, most birds adapted to attain the necessary requirements for flight.

Birds date back to the age of dinosaurs and reptiles. The first feathered fossil found, named Archaeopteryx, shows birds have been around for millions of years. Can you imagine a flying dinosaur? The next time you have an opportunity to look at the lower leg of a chicken, notice the reptilian scales on it. All birds have these leg scales. To this day, there is disagreement between paleontologists (scientists who study dinosaurs) and ornithologists (scientists who study birds). Did birds change from reptiles and evolve to what they are now? Or were birds already there, evolving and changing? Did they go from the ground to the trees or from the trees to the ground? Recently there are new feathered fossils coming from Asia. Will these new fossils prove who is right, or is there still a missing link? We don't yet know the answers.

Adaptation has produced approximately 800 species of birds in the United States and over 8,600 species of birds in the world today. All this adaptation has resulted in extremes of bird species, including colorful parrots in the tropical rain forests, and penguins, which can't fly, living in extremely cold conditions.

Skeletal

Some birds, such as ostriches, are ground dwellers; others, such as terns, are fliers. To enable birds to attain flight, the keel or breastbone had to change, allowing the proper muscle attachment with the wing. Leg and wing structures changed along with bone size and bone density. In most birds, the bones became hollow giving them less weight. The reduced weight enabled muscles to get them airborne and maintain flight.

Feathers / Plumage

A feather has a hollow cylinder, or calamus (quill), whose base embeds in a skin follicle. Its flat, tapered shape consists of a tuft of barbs and barbules that actually hook to each other. The act of preening grooms and realigns these barbules back to functioning condition. Many birds, such as ducks, have an oil gland near the base of their tail. Preening allows these birds to add oil to their feathers to keep water from entering. Feathers also trap air to keep the bird warm and insulate it from the elements. The overall plumage gives the bird its color, shape and ability to fly. The flight feathers give necessary flexibility and stiffness for flying. Tail feathers are the rudders that allow birds to steer. In the case of the woodpeckers, stiff tail feathers allow them to brace against trees while pecking. Variety in adaptation gave birds the ability to live in a multitude of habitats.

Other Features

Bird size, region and climate in which they live affect metabolism and foods they eat. Their heart, blood vessels, sex organs and other internal features also evolved to fit their habitat.

It is critical for many birds to have strong lungs to capture oxygen needed for muscles in long-distance migrations. We all know that ducks and geese are strong fliers and travel long distances each spring and fall. The arctic tern migrates from the North Pole to the South Pole, and returns to the North Pole each year. That's a lot of flight miles. But, the overall champion of migration is the hummingbird. When size is factored in, this tiny bird puts out more energy in migration than all other birds.

As time went on, a bird's mouth, tongue and bill also changed. A cardinal has a beak that allows it to crack and eat seeds. Insect eaters usually have longer bills to allow easy removal of insects from crevices. A mallard's bill allows it to grab water vegetation and chew its food, and a hummingbird's long tongue allows it to slurp nectar from its favorite flowers.

Adaptation also altered their feet and toes. Ducks and geese have webbed feet for swimming. A woodpecker's opposing toes allow it to climb, and some ground birds like ostriches have big muscular legs for running. Can you imagine an ostrich on the side of a tree? Better yet, how about a pheasant swimming in a lake. The majority of birds became passerines (perching birds) like finches and chickadees.

Senses

A bird's sight is either monocular, binocular, or a combination of both. Monocular sight (robin, woodcock) allows birds to see to the side and somewhat to the rear, but it makes seeing in front more difficult. This protects the bird from rear attacks but it must tilt its head to see what's in front. Binocular sight (owls) allows great frontal vision and depth perception, but poor rear or side vision. This forces it to turn its head and look directly at what it wants to see, just like humans.

A good sense of hearing is another achievement of birds. In owls, the hearing is acentric. The left ear is different from the right. One eardrum is ahead of and aligned lower than the other eardrum. Receiving sound differently from each ear gives the bird the ability to zero in on its prey at night without relying on sight alone.

Smell doesn't seem to be one of their better senses, although scientists have found the turkey vulture possesses a very keen sense of smell. Scientists continue to explore this ability in birds.

We must also consider propagation and how color, number, and egg-laying frequency come into play. Some birds are very colorful, while others are drab. This is usually because males (who are colorful) use their plumage to attract females for breeding. In contrast, the females (who are drab) use their drabness to camouflage themselves from predators, such as raptors (birds of prey) or cats, during incubation and rearing of their young. Scientists call this sexual dimorphism. Ornithologists are now questioning this theory too.

Without these adaptations, our feathered friends would not have survived here on Earth. Would we humans be able to survive the Ice Age and all the environmental changes as they did? Birds are proven experts at evolving to live in specific environmental niches, and become masters of: running (turkeys), flight (terns), swimming (geese), gliding (owls), soaring (eagles) and eating (hummingbirds).

Where & How to Find Birds

The key to finding birds or any animal is finding a habitat or combination of habitats that provide their four basic needs:
1. food
2. water
3. shelter
4. a place to raise young

Some of these habitats are riparian, forest, lakes, meadows, pastures, lawns, hedgerows, your backyard and, most of all, transition zones. Birds, like humans, require certain things to sustain life. Ducks like water, woodpeckers like trees. You wouldn't see a goose in the woods anymore than you would see a nuthatch in the water. Even though each bird's requirements differ, all need the four basics. So, key in on the habitat that provides for a specific bird's needs. Some like seeds (cardinals); others like insects (warblers); some eat fish (herons); and some will consume seeds, nuts or insects (chickadees). Concentrate on their needs, habitat preferences, and food requirements, and you will find birds.

Bird Identification

Field Identification Guides

A bird identification field guide is probably the one item of most value to bird lovers. (See page 146 for field guide recommendations.) Guides are easy-to-use and they complement the use of binoculars, photography, video and sound taping. Their small size makes them easy to pack and handle during hiking, biking or while paddling a canoe or kayak.

Some of the newer guides have photographs rather than an artist's rendition of the bird. For many people, the photo style seems more realistic. Either style will work. Guides show what a particular bird looks like, the differences between males and females, the immature, and morphs (color phases) of a specific bird and a bird's range in summer, winter or year-round. Also, the guides describe the bird's favorite habitat and where they prefer to live.

Field identification guides also tell if birds come to a bird box, what kind of nest they like to build or take over, and number, color and size of eggs they lay. Best of all, if you feed birds, field guides tell what kinds of food each bird prefers and whether they normally come to feeders.

Bird Sounds

Some guides describe a bird's song, or how birds call, and the manner or reason for calling. For example, in addition to vocalizing, woodpeckers drum or tattoo on the side of a tree to announce their intentions to a mate.

Because a lot of bird identification is done by sound, get some good audiotapes or CDs with recorded bird sounds. Recordings can be purchased or borrowed from a library. As you listen, they describe which bird made each sound. Some of the better ones describe more than one sound per bird, and include the differences between males and females. Clocks are available with bird pictures at each hour position. The corresponding bird call plays on the hour.

For those who have a VCR, there are excellent videotapes available that guide you through identification. The National Audubon Society and Stokes tapes are good choices.

If you have a computer with a CD reader, there are some excellent programs that show, describe, and in some cases, quiz you on birds. They require a lot of computer memory, so verify that your computer can handle the memory required. Some of the better CDs are by Thayer Birding Software, Peterson and the National Audubon Society. The Peterson CD is available for PC or Apple computers.

Questions to Ask as you Try to Identify a Bird

Key in on the habitat where you see a particular bird, and on the foods that this habitat produces. When you do this, look for the birds that could be there, and forget about the birds that shouldn't be there. In other words, don't expect to see shorebirds in a forest habitat.

Develop a process that works for you. Perhaps, make a mental note or write down and draw all the characteristics you can identify from the list below. Then check in your field identification guide to identify the species.

Habitat: Is it on land or in the water?
Size: Is it big or small?
Shape: Differences of legs, tails, bills, etc.
Color: Is it one color or more than one color?
Plumage: Is it brightly colored or drab?
Markings: Are there any unusual patches or marks?
Song or call: What kind of voice does it have?
Where is it living: Is it in a tree hole or on the ground?
Silhouette: How does it appear against the background?
Flight style: Does it hover or glide?
Flight pattern: Does it fly in certain formations?
Behavior: What is it doing? Is it hopping, climbing up or down, swimming?
Food: What is it eating?

Use the diagram below to learn the terms commonly used to describe parts of birds in field identification guides.

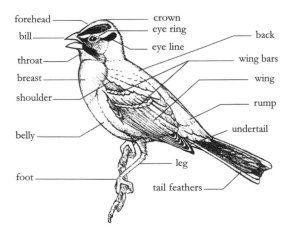

forehead
bill
throat
breast
shoulder
belly
foot
crown
eye ring
eye line
leg
tail feathers
back
wing bars
wing
rump
undertail

Bird Finder List

Many factors, including wind direction, temperature, time of day, food supplies elsewhere, etc. influence your chances of seeing specific birds. Here are some recommendations for places and times of year when your chances of seeing or hearing a specific species are enhanced.

Bird Species	Where	When
Accipiter hawks	Braddock Bay Beaver Meadow Audubon Center	Year-round
Bitterns	Montezuma NWR Iroquois NWR	Summer, Fall
Blackbirds	Conesus Inlet F&WMA	Spring, Summer, Fall
Bluebirds	Black Creek Park	Spring, Summer
Buteo hawks	Braddock Bay Black Creek Park	Year-round
Cardinals	Greece Canal Park Beaver Meadow Audubon Center	Year-round
Chickadees	Mendon Ponds Park-Birdsong Trail	Year-round
Diving ducks	Dunkirk Harbor Buckhorn Island State Park	Spring, Fall, Winter
Eagles	Montezuma NWR Iroquois NWR	Spring, Fall
Egrets	Montezuma NWR Iroquois NWR	Summer
Evening grosbeaks	Allegany State Park	Spring, Fall
Finches	Chenango Valley State Park	Spring, Summer, Fall
Geese	Montezuma NWR Iroquois NWR	Spring, Summer, Fall
Goldfinches	Green Lakes State Park Black Creek Park	Spring, Summer, Fall
Gulls/terns	Dunkirk Harbor Buckhorn Island State Park	Year-round
Herons	Conesus Inlet F&WMA Montezuma NWR	Spring, Summer, Fall
Kingfishers	Chenango Valley State Park	Spring, Summer, Fall
Kinglets	Keeney Swamp State Forest	Spring, Fall
Nuthatches	Mendon Ponds Park-Birdsong Trail	Year-round
Owls	Braddock Bay Raptor Research Trail Allegany State Park	Spring, Fall

Puddle ducks	Montezuma NWR	Spring, Summer, Fall
	Iroquois NWR	
Rose-breasted grosbeaks	Allegany State Park	Spring, Summer
Scarlet tanangers	Ossian State Forest	Spring, Summer, Fall
	Allegany State Park	
Shorebirds	Montezuma NWR	Spring, Summer, Fall
Thrushes	Allegany State Park	Spring, Summer
	Chenango Valley State Park	
Titmice	Mendon Ponds Park-Birdsong Trail	Year-round
Turkey vultures	Hi Tor WMA	Spring, Summer, Fall
	Allegany State Park	
Turkeys / grouse	Ossian State Forest	Year-round
	Allegany State Park	
Vireos	Chenango Valley State Park	Summer
Warblers	Montezuma Esker Brook Trail	Spring, Fall
Woodpeckers	Ossian State Forest	Year-round
	Beaver Lake Nature Center	
Wrens	Allegany State Park	Spring, Summer, Fall
	Beaver Lake Nature Center	

Most of the trails and waterways are excellent for year-round birding. The following are known for the visitation of seasonal species:

Where	Spring	Summer	Fall	Winter
Allegany State Park	X	X	X	
Beaver Lake Nature Center	X	X	X	
Black Creek Park	X	X	X	
Braddock Bay Area	X		X	
Buckhorn Island State Park	X		X	X
Chenango Valley State Park	X	X	X	
Conesus Inlet F&WMA	X	X	X	
Dunkirk Harbor	X		X	X
Green Lakes State Park	X	X	X	
Hi Tor WMA	X	X	X	
Iroquois NWR	X	X	X	
Keeney Swamp State Forest	X	X	X	
Montezuma NWR	X	X	X	
Ossian State Forest	X	X	X	

To Enhance Your Enjoyment

Binoculars

I highly recommend using binoculars. They enable you to magnify your subject for better viewing. Before purchasing binoculars, ask yourself these questions:

- Where and how do I intend to use them?
- What kind of punishment are they likely to receive?
- Is their size or weight an issue to consider?

Binoculars come in two styles. The first is the Porro prism. These are generally shorter, and they have wider, offset front (objective) lenses. The second is the Roof prism. They are usually longer, having the front and rear lenses in-line with each other. Both have distinct advantages, but the Porro prism models tend to be less expensive.

The purpose of these lenses is to gather and project as much light as possible to your eyes. This is especially important in low light or shady conditions, where much bird activity takes place. Better binoculars come with more coatings on the lenses and more precisely polished glass. This allows them to gather light with less distortion. The better the lens, the more they cost.

Most people have different levels of vision in each eye; therefore, it's helpful to get binoculars that let you adjust lenses separately. After you adjust for your sight, merely focus in on your subject.

You will notice that binoculars have numbers on them; for example, 7 x 35. The first number (in this case 7) is the amount of power, or a magnification seven times greater than normal vision. The second number (in this case 35) is the number of millimeters in diameter of the front objective lens.

If you divide these two numbers (7 into 35 =5), this gives you the exit pupil diameter in millimeters. A higher exit pupil diameter e.g. 7 x 42 (7 into 42 = 6 mm) or 8 x 40 (8 into 40 = 5 mm) will give better results than a lower number by allowing more light to enter your eyes. Although some of the newer and better binoculars, e. g. 8 x 20 (8 into 20 = 2.5 mm), or 10 x 23 (10 into 23 = 2.3 mm), do give acceptable results in favorable light conditions.

My personal feeling is that it's better not to buy binoculars with too high a power of magnification. Once you get beyond an 8 or 10 power, the binoculars are harder to keep steady (unless used with a tripod). They also magnify particles or haze, and distort things such as heat waves coming off the ground or water.

A third group of numbers, such as 350ft/1000yards, describes the field of view. This means that at 1000 yards, you have a field of view of 350 feet. This is a basic view width. There are wider widths, e.g. 500ft/1000yards or 550ft/1000yards. A wider field of view makes it easier and faster to find your subject.

Some binoculars have eyecups for people who wear eyeglasses. By folding the rubber cups the eyes get closer to the viewing lens for better vision.

Ask other birders what types or models they use; then shop around and find a pair that fits your budget. You do not have to spend hundreds of dollars, but remember the better the lenses and light gathering capability, the more they will cost. There are good binoculars for around a hundred dollars. I recommend beginning birders or nature lovers start with a smaller and lighter pocket size model. As you gain more experience, you can step up to better binoculars. I still use my pocket binoculars most often because they're easy to carry. Any binoculars are better than none.

Photography

If you want to enjoy birding and nature at a different level, consider photography. Pictures give you the ability to share a moment or memory with someone else. Cameras come in many styles, qualities and price ranges. Many come with automatic features, but buy one that lets you override those features. That way you can do manual adjustments for more flexibility during picture taking. The most commonly used format is the 35-mm camera. These range from the single-use and point-and-shoot cameras at the low end, to the SLR (single lens reflex) at the upper end of quality and price. With a SLR camera, you can change lenses quickly, and what you see in the sight window is what the camera sees. There is a mirror that flips out of the way when you press the button, letting the image continue to the film.

Other than quality film, the lens is the most important item in producing good pictures. As with binoculars, the better the lens the more the camera will cost. Many cameras come with a fixed lens (e.g. 50-mm). These lenses are good for general use or distance shots, which represent the biggest percentage of photography for beginning birders or nature lovers. They are light and easy to pack or carry. On the other hand, if you don't mind the weight or want to expand your pleasure, you can get additional lenses. One to consider would be a telephoto (70 x 210) lens that allows you to zoom in on your subject. If you put a 2X converter on the 70 x 210 lens, you double it to a 140 x 420 for more magnification. It saves buying an additional lens, but you will lose some quality and light capability.

For close-up pictures, a macro lens can't be beat. Better yet, get a macro-telephoto lens. It lets you get very close to your subject, or zoom in, and also accepts a 2X converter. This gives your camera a wide range of capabilities, from very close (bird nests) to a scene that is far away.

Getting close to a bird or nest is extremely difficult. Sometimes I use a tripod, flash and shutter release. I set up the shot, walk away, wait for the shot to evolve, and click. A good camera store can show you cameras with these features.

After choosing the camera, lenses and gadgets that make photography fun, the most important item to consider is your film. A slow film speed (100) gives better quality. The photos are less grainy (hazy). But a slow film speed requires a lot of light and sometimes minimal movement. Because of either poor light conditions (even with a flash), or the quickness of birds, you may need a faster film speed (400) to capture birds without a blurred image. In some instances, you may want that blurred effect. It's your photo, and that's what makes photography fun. In other words: take it your way. Most importantly, always use quality film and processing. A good camera is only as good as the film and processing used.

If you know you are going to take a lot of photographs, or plan to show them to a group, you should consider slides (transparencies). Slides are almost half the cost of prints and can be very impressive when projected. An inter-negative can be made from a slide, to produce prints and enlargements. Doing this will diminish the quality slightly, but it provides another option.

You may want to make your own prints or enlarge (increase the size of) your photos. To do this, you need to take a course in photography, developing and printmaking. I've had a lot of fun doing this, but it requires a darkroom and equipment. There are places where you can rent a darkroom or equipment. Many photo processors now offer enlargements. With scanners available today, you can scan transparencies and negatives into a computer to produce prints, enlargements, and electronic files. Keep in mind the larger you blow-up a print or the faster the film speed, the grainier your pictures.

Avid photographers like to use a 4 x 5-format camera. They tend to be more expensive, heavier and require a bit more experience. Their biggest advantage is having a bigger negative size. This bigger negative results in nice big photos that enlarge to higher quality, less grainy prints. If you like taking scenic and nature shots, or want to do your own higher quality prints, then this format might be for you.

You may want to consider the newer APS (Advanced Photo System) camera. The APS is a negative film base (like 35-mm), but in a 24-mm format. The results are the same, but the cameras tend to be smaller, lighter and more streamlined. They are user friendly. You drop the film in, and the camera does the rest. You load it, aim it, click it, unload, and process the film. The APS format requires a different type of film process-ing than the 35-mm, but most processing labs offer this service.

For those who want the newest in cameras, digital is the way to go. It will give you many options that are not available in other formats. These cameras take quality stills, and in some cases, acceptable motion pictures. Many are made to use with your computer. Just load the disc or floppy into the cam-era, select your options and away you go. When finished, insert the disc in your computer and enjoy. You can make copies, prints, and in some cases, enlargements. You can make presentations and show them through your monitor, project them to a screen or to a TV. Best of all, you can send them to a company, friend or relative over the Internet. You must have the right hardware and software, but just think of the possibilities!

Video

Many people enjoy taking their own videos, using 8 mm, VHS or digital formats. The natural world is the perfect place to use video. The scene is set up and waiting for you. The newer camcorders are small, light and easy to use. Plus, they record excellent sound. Note: If you are talking as you take your video, don't talk too loud or you'll cover up the sounds you're recording. A microphone that detaches from the recorder can elim-inate this problem. Also, as with cameras, be mindful of light conditions, and never move fast or pan your subject too quickly. Here again is where a tripod could help steady your recording. Some recorders allow you to transfer video to your VCR or load motion or individual pictures into your computer. As with cameras, better recorders with multiple features, cost more.

Audio

Those who enjoy the sounds of nature and birds should definitely try recording their own audiotapes. This can be difficult to do at times, especially if there is extraneous noise. Although small hand-held recorders will work, the better recorders tend to be cumbersome, heavy and require a lot of battery power. But if you're looking for a challenge, this might be fun to try. There is enough variety in the sounds of nature to keep you busy for a long time. I remember many occasions, as I paddled my canoe, wishing I could record the sounds I heard as well as photographing the scenery. There's something about the sounds of nature in a very pristine environment that stirs my soul.

Synergy With Gardening

Birding (watching and feeding) is the second rated *fun activity* enjoyed in America, second only to gardening. Yet, if you think about it, there's a common bond between gardens and birds. Gardens need water, so do birds. Gardens have destructive pests. Some birds eat the pests that otherwise may infest a garden. After pollination, plants grow and produce seeds. Some birds eat the seeds. Can you see how it works; how everything coexists? Also, gardeners usually like birding, and birders like to garden? They go together well.

Keeping a Log

If you like to watch birds, try recording or logging what you see. Write down the species of birds you observe. How many are there? Where are they? When did you observe them? Other interesting information may include the weather and what they're consuming. There is a personal log on page 144 to get you started.

Better yet, consider joining Cornell Lab of Ornithology projects like Project Feeder Watch or Birds in Forested Landscapes. Collect information and report it to the Lab. The information is shared with other birders and used to keep track of bird populations. Another good program is the House Finch Disease Survey, where you observe the number of birds that are suffering from an eye disease, and provide the data to the Lab.

These programs are excellent for school classroom or science projects. For more information, visit their web site at: http://birds.cornell.edu.

Monitoring Birds

Some people enjoy participating in bird monitoring programs. For instance, they put up houses on a bluebird trail, then watch, document, perhaps band, and share the information with local clubs or agencies such as The Birdhouse Network. Birds, such as turkeys, bluebirds, ducks and geese have made a great recovery in numbers because people have gotten involved and helped them out.

Safety & Environment

When we go outdoors, we have to think about how we interact with the natural world. This book will help you with the *where* and *how* of birding, but it's your responsibility to proceed in a safe and thoughtful manner.

You need to plan for safety, whenever going on an outing. Create a personal checklist to gather and check your equipment. Be sure all equipment (canoes, bikes, packs, etc.) is in proper working condition. Check your equipment when you put it away, and again when you are ready to use it. If you are borrowing or renting equipment, make extra sure it is in good condition, and know how to use it.

Nature is constantly changing, so think about the season or potential weather conditions and factor them into your equipment planning. Remember that getting there and returning from the outing should be included in your safety plan.

Whether you go alone or with companions (a safer choice), be sure to tell someone else where you're going and when you intend to return. Although the trips in this book do not tend to be difficult or long (generally an hour, to less than a day), everyone's ability level is different. Start with an easier trip and work up to the more challenging ones.

Consider getting some emergency training. Your training should include first aid and CPR (cardio pulmonary resuscitation), and always take a first aid kit with you.

Be sure to take proper clothing for a range of conditions. Bring food and, most importantly, water. Good planning includes a little extra rationing of food and water. Humans can survive up to a month without food but only two to three days without water. Always have plenty of good water with you. As a precaution, consider carrying iodine tablets or a water filter. If you don't have these, take matches and a suitable container to boil any questionable water.

Other things to consider taking along:
- This book with its maps
- Compass and additional maps (know how to use them)
- Hat and possibly gloves (especially for cold or winter outings)
- Sunscreen and sunglasses
- Sanitary needs
- Proper footwear and extra socks for the conditions
- Field identification guide
- Binoculars
- Camera and film

- Insect repellent
- Matches or lighter
- Other personal items for the conditions

Water Safety

Canoes and kayaks are made from a variety of materials that affect their weight and durability. They are designed for specific types of water conditions, such as white water vs. flat water. Each canoe handles and maneuvers differently, so familiarize yourself with the craft before you leave on a trip.

If canoeing or kayaking:
- Everyone must always wear an approved life vest/jacket or PFD (personal flotation device)
- Get off or stay off the water when lightning is present or imminent
- Take along extra paddles
- Pack all gear in waterproof bags and tie them securely to your craft

If you capsize in open water, stay with and grab onto the canoe or kayak. It will stay afloat. On the other hand, if you're in rapids or fast water, position yourself upstream and far away from the canoe or kayak. It could hit you if you're too close. Plus, if you get tangled or wedged between an object and the craft, the force of the water against it could be disastrous. Head downstream, feet first with your knees slightly bent to absorb the impact from rocks or other objects. This is when you'll be thankful you wore that life vest. It will keep you afloat while you're in the water.

Guidelines

These outings are not intended to be hard or long. They are intended to be fun, educational and adventurous. Your enjoyment will increase if you follow these simple guidelines:
- Be quiet (you will see more wildlife)
- Stay on the given course
- Use good judgment
- Respect other people and wildlife
- Don't pick plants
- Carry out what you bring in (if possible take out what others didn't carry out)

You will return safely and have completed the trip with minimum impact to our environment.

Extended Outings

Some of the outings in this book can be extended, combined or done as an overnight adventure. But, to do so without the proper skills or knowledge is not using good judgment, especially during the winter. You can get information from books and magazines pertaining to outdoor skills at a library. Classes dealing with canoeing, camping, backpacking and the wilderness are taught at local swimming pools, museums, schools and adventure outfitters.

If you want to plan an extended outing, here are some additional items to consider:

- A good backpack (if a daypack is not big enough)
- Fire or stove and cooking supplies (check if fire and camping permits are required)
- Sleeping gear
- Medications
- Flashlight and extra batteries
- Additional personal items

Whether walking, bicycling or paddling, the safety processes described and the tips given should always be followed. Remember that you have a responsibility to yourself, others and the environment. Enjoy your adventure safely and think of your impact on wildlife. Respect your environment and it will be there for enjoyment another day.

Most of all, take the time to get out and enjoy the wonders of nature surrounding us. This guide gets you started at some great locations.

Routes in the
Far West

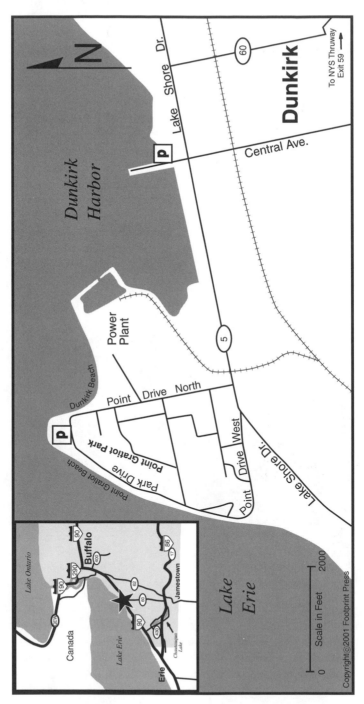

Dunkirk Harbor & Point Gratiot Park

1.

Dunkirk Harbor and Point Gratiot Park

Location: Dunkirk, Chautauqua County

Directions: **Dunkirk Harbor:** Take the NYS Thruway to exit 59. Turn on Route 60 North and proceed 2 miles to the waterfront. Turn left on Route 5 then right on Central Avenue. The pier and parking area are at the north end of Central Avenue.

Point Gratiot Park: It's a short 0.5-mile drive to the west along Lake Shore Drive. Then turn right on Point Drive North to Point Gratiot Park. Or, turn right on Point Drive West and continue onto Park Drive for a one-way drive through the park.

Admission: Free

Trail Length: A few hundred yards on the pier

There are no trails in Point Gratiot Park but you can walk among the trees or along the shore.

Time To Hike: Approximately 30 minutes at each location

Trail Markings: None

Difficulty Level: 1

Birds Likely Seen: Ducks, gulls, Canada geese, coots, nuthatches, red-headed woodpeckers, chickadees and robins

Other Park Uses: Picnicking, sport activities and swimming at the beach

Contact: City of Dunkirk
342 Central Avenue, Dunkirk, NY 14048
(716) 366-0452

Dunkirk Harbor:

Dunkirk Harbor is located on the southeast shore of Lake Erie. A large Niagara Mohawk power plant discharges warm water into the harbor which prevents the area from freezing in winter. The open water provides a winter feeding and resting habitat for large numbers of gulls and ducks, including thousands of mergansers and hundreds of Bonaparte's gulls.

Route: From the pier parking lot, walk the pier, and enjoy the variety and numbers of gulls, ducks and geese. You're likely to see species of diving ducks such as merganser, buffle-head, scaup and golden-eye. These are less common in western New York than the puddle ducks typically found in marshes such as mallard and teal. Watch carefully for tundra swans, red-heads, canvasbacks, old squaws, double-crested cormorants, loons, grebes, and scoters.

Point Gratiot Park:

Point Gratiot Park is a city park across the street from the US Coast Guard Station and lighthouse. In the spring many songbirds gather at nearby Point Gratiot and wait for good weather before crossing Lake Erie. The park has a resident population of red-headed woodpeckers and makes a perfect place for birds to rest during migration. Peak times for sightings are around the second and third weeks of May.

Route: Many people aim their binoculars from the warmth of their cars along the road within the park. Or, feel free to wander among the trees or along the shore to get different perspectives.

Date:

Birds Seen:

Other Observations:

Allegany State Park

Allegany State Park is southeast of Buffalo, near Salamanca and adjacent to the Seneca Indian Reservation. The city of Salamanca is actually on the reservation. Obviously, the Allegany area is rich in Indian culture. The park also borders Pennsylvania and the Allegheny National Forest.

Allegany State Park is New York State's largest four-season park and is a hiking and camping paradise. The park is great for road and mountain biking. It has 91 miles of groomed snowmobile trails, winterized cabins and cross-country ski trails for winter activity. The Allegheny River and Kinzua Dam near Warren, PA, create a large open water reservoir that backs up almost to the city of Salamanca and provides great boating and fishing. But, the big open water can get pretty rough, so it can be dangerous for canoeists. If you plan to fish, be sure you have the proper licenses, especially around the PA/NY border.

The park has several entrances. Red House (exit 19 off I-86) and Quaker (exit 18 off I-86) are the main ones. The administration office and park facilities are at Red House Area along with a taxidermy museum and park information displays. At the administration building, you can pick up maps of the bicycle and hiking trails. Both Red House Lake and Quaker Lake have beaches where swimming and canoeing are allowed. To camp in the campsites or rent a cabin, you must register by calling 1-800-456-CAMP.

The park and surrounding areas are wonderful for bird observations and nature encounters. Its size and diversity make this park an excellent area for birding, whether you're around water, on a trail or on a bike. The park has three main roads: ASP1, ASP2 and ASP3. Each road has site number signs along its edge to help you find specific spots within the park. For example, a good area for night-time owls is on ASP2, at site #32. A good area for spring warblers is around the fire tower area on the Mount Tuscarora Trail, or around site #56 off ASP3. One of the better riparian areas is on France Brook Road, especially near site #30. This is also a good place to see a beaver lodge and dam. At dusk you may also see the active beavers. Beavers can also be found at Red House Lake near the headquarters.

Additional trails in Allegany State Park that are good for birding:

Trail Name	Distance	Difficulty	Use
Bear Caves Trail	4.0 miles	3	Hiking only
Mt. Tuscarora Trail	5.0 miles	3	Hiking only
Three Sisters Trail	2.5 miles	2	Hiking only
Osgood Trail	2.5 miles	2	Hiking only
North Country Trail	18.0 miles	3	Hiking only

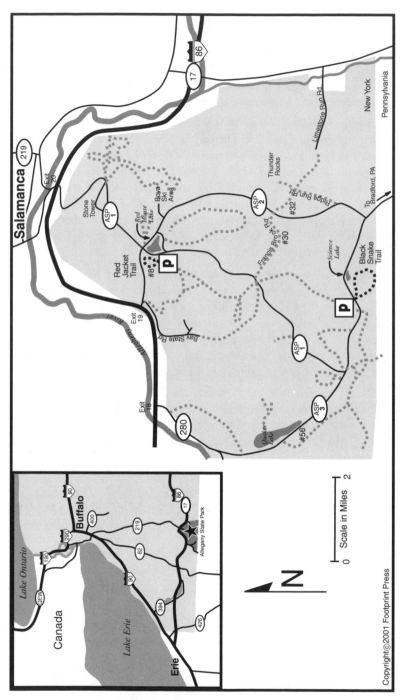

Allegany State Park

Copyright©2001 Footprint Press

2.
Allegany State Park — Red Jacket Trail

Location: Red House Area off ASP 1, Cattaraugus County

Directions: Take exit 19 off I-86 and head south into Allegany State Park. Turn right on ASP 1. The administration building (with parking) will be on the right. The trail (Trail #8) entrance is located directly behind the administration building.

Admission: $6/vehicle is charged to enter the park between 9 AM and 5 PM from Memorial Day through Labor Day

Trail Length: A 0.4-mile loop off the 2-mile Red Jacket Trail

Time To Hike: 20 minutes

Trail Conditions: Trail has some rocks and roots

Trail Surface: Dirt

Trail Markings: Arrows painted on trees

Difficulty Level: 2

Birds Likely Seen: Chickadees, nuthatches, woodpeckers, titmice, wrens and brown creepers

Other Park Uses: Biking, swimming, hiking, fishing, horseback riding, hunting and camping

Contact: Allegany State Park
2373 ASP#1, Salamanca, NY 14779
(716) 354-9101

Route: Start behind the headquarters building. Turn right at the Red Jacket Trail sign and proceed straight ahead. Bear right when the trail separates and follow the trail for 0.1 mile until you see two old, abandoned ski jump towers and a rock wall. Just past the wall, turn left. As the trail loops back, head diagonally up the hill and back to the starting point. This is a short trail, but it will give you an appreciation of what the park has to offer and whet your appetite to explore additional trails within Allegany State Park.

Date:

Birds Seen:

Other Observations:

3.

Allegany State Park — Black Snake Trail

Location:	South end of park, off ASP3, Cattaraugus County
Directions:	From Exit 18 off I-86, follow NY 280 south to the Allegany State Park Entrance. Follow ASP3 past Quaker Lake, then past ASP1 and Coon Run Road. The Black Snake parking lot and trail (Trail #3) entrance will be on the south side of ASP3.
Admission:	$6/vehicle is charged to enter the park between 9 AM and 5 PM from Memorial Day through Labor Day
Trail Length:	3 miles
Time To Hike:	About 1.5 hours
Trail Conditions:	Hilly, sometimes wet with roots and rocks
Trail Surface:	Dirt and grass
Trail Markings:	Arrows and blazes painted on trees
Trail Difficulty:	2, 3
Birds Likely Seen:	Woodpeckers (pileated), nuthatches, chickadees, turkeys, grouse, blue jays, wrens and cardinals
Other Park Uses:	Biking, hiking, swimming, fishing, horseback riding, hunting and camping
Contact:	Allegany State Park 2373 ASP#1, Salamanca, NY 14779 (716) 354-9101

Route: Follow the trail from the parking lot. Then bear right (where the trail separates) and head southeast. You'll progressively climb higher and cross a few water drainages. The majority of the trail is open woods. Eventually you'll reach the top, and the trail will level off. About one-third of the way along the trail, you'll come to the Pennsylvania state line. Look for the concrete geological survey marker (#174) a few feet in on the right side of the trail.

The trail will start to get easier as you head downhill. At about 1.25 miles the trail will start to loop to the left and head north. You'll pass what appears to be a bear's den. There are many bears in this park. For the last 0.25 mile the trail will bend left and lead back to the starting point. Watch for deer along the route. Also, listen for grouse drumming and look for owl pellets as you hike.

Date:

Birds Seen:

Other Observations:

Routes near Buffalo

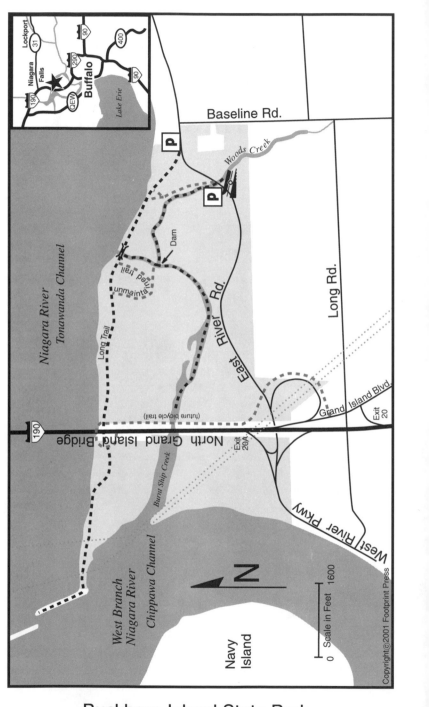

Buckhorn Island State Park

4.

Buckhorn Island State Park — Long Trail

Location:	Grand Island, Erie County
Directions:	If heading south on I-190, take exit 20A. Turn left and follow East River Road to the parking areas. If traveling north on I-190, take exit 20. Turn left (W) on Grand Island Boulevard, then left (S) on Long Road. At the end, turn right (N) on West River Parkway. This will turn into East River Road and lead to the parking areas.
Admission:	Free (but there is a toll charge when crossing the Grand Island bridge)
Trail Length:	About 5 miles round trip
Time To Hike:	Approximately 2 hours
Trail Conditions:	Sometimes wet
Trail Surface:	Dirt trail, some concrete and stone
Trail Markings:	None
Trail Difficulty:	1
Birds Likely Seen:	Gulls, ducks, geese, woodpeckers, nuthatches, herons, and chickadees
Other Park Uses:	Hiking, biking, canoeing and cross-country skiing
Contact:	Buckhorn Island State Park c/o Beaver Island State Park 2136 West Oakfield Road, Grand Island, NY 14072 (716) 773-3271

Buckhorn Island is an 895-acre parcel of meadow, woods and marsh separated from Grand Island by Burnt Ship Creek and Woods Creek. The Long Trail that leads along the Niagara River provides good views of the river and other shoreline features.

In December 1996, the Niagara River corridor was officially designated an Important Bird Area (IBA). What makes this area special is that 19 of the world's 45 gull species overwinter here. It is also a good place to see rafts of diving ducks and get an occasional glimpse of the harlequin duck. The river corridor makes a perfect place for birds to rest during migration.

The first parking area you'll pass, near Woods Creek, is accessible to the handicapped for fishing and has a canoe launch. The second parking area, closer to Baseline Road, can accommodate additional cars.

Route: The walking trail has a variety of things to see, including the northern Grand Island bridge. Start the trail from either parking lot. Watch for gulls as you walk and see how many different species of you can identify. Also watch for rafts of diving ducks, such as scaup, buffle-heads, golden-eyes and occasionally canvasbacks, which use this area. When you get to the west end of the island, turn around and follow the trail back to the parking area.

Date:

Birds Seen:

Other Observations:

5.

Buckhorn Island State Park — Woods Creek

Location: Grand Island, Erie County

Directions: If heading south on I-190, take exit 20A. Turn left and follow East River Road to the Woods Creek parking area. If traveling north on I-190, take exit 20. Turn left (W) on Grand Island Boulevard, then left (S) on Long Road. At the end, turn right (N) on West River Parkway. This will turn into East River Road.

Admission: Free (but there is a toll charge when crossing the Grand Island bridge)

Route Length: About 0.7-mile on Woods Creek and 0.7-mile on Burnt Ship Creek each way

Time To Canoe: Approximately 2 hours or more

Route Conditions: Narrow stream and marsh

Route Markings: None

Route Difficulty: 1

Birds Likely Seen: Gulls, ducks, geese, woodpeckers, nuthatches, herons, and chickadees

Other Park Uses: Hiking, biking, fishing and cross-country skiing

Contact: Buckhorn Island State Park
c/o Beaver Island State Park
2136 West Oakfield Road, Grand Island, NY 14072
(716) 773-3271

Buckhorn Island is an 895-acre parcel of meadow, woods and marsh separated from Grand Island by Burnt Ship Creek and Woods Creek. You can explore this Important Bird Area on foot via the Long Trail (see page 45) or hop in your kayak or canoe for a water-level view from Woods Creek and the Burnt Ship Creek marsh. Bring along the fishing gear if you want to catch dinner while birdwatching.

Route: From the parking area, carry your canoe across East River Road to launch. Head left (N) watching for various ducks, gulls and geese as you paddle, and peer into the trees for woodland birds, maybe even an osprey. At a bend in the creek you'll see a small dam (waste weir). You can continue on Woods Creek to the Niagara River, or portage around the dam and explore the marsh area of Burnt Ship Creek. The Niagara River is a swift channel so it's not recommended for canoes and kayaks.

Date:

Birds Seen:

Other Observations:

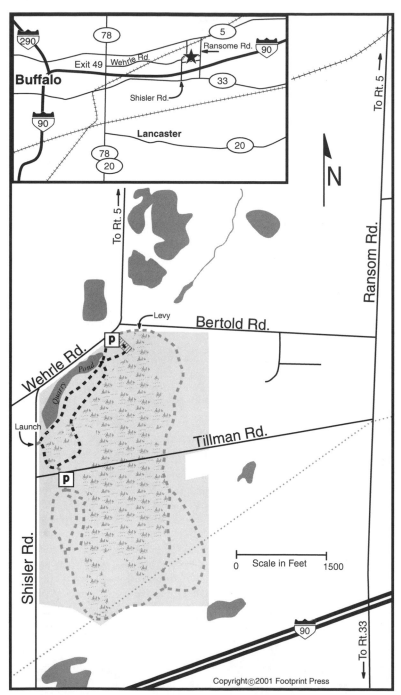

Tillman Road Wildlife Management Area

6.
Tillman Road Wildlife Management Area
— Trail

Location:	Clarence, Erie County
Directions:	Take the NYS Thruway to exit 49. Head south on Route 78 to Route 33. Head east on Route 33. Turn left (N) on Shisler Road. Turn right on Wehrle Road and the parking area will be ahead on your right.
Admission:	Free
Trail Length:	About 1.25-mile loop
Time To Hike:	Approximately 60 minutes
Trail Conditions:	Sometimes wet
Trail Surface:	Wooden boardwalk and woodchip trail
Trail Markings:	None
Trail Difficulty:	1
Birds Likely Seen:	Woodpeckers, nuthatches, chickadees, blackbirds, turkey vultures, meadowlarks, goldfinches, herons, bitterns, rails, grebes, ducks and geese
Other Park Uses:	Photography, cross-country skiing, and fishing in Quarry Pond only
Contact:	NYS DEC Region 9 Tillman Road Wildlife Management Area 270 Michigan Avenue, Buffalo, NY (716) 851-7010

The Tillman Road WMA has 235 acres of wet lowlands containing a marsh, open water, deciduous swamp, grass fields and hardwood forest. The 80-acre cattail marsh attracts large numbers of waterfowl during the spring and fall migrations. They can be viewed from the boardwalk (which is handicapped accessible) at the Wehrle Road entrance. Canada geese, mallards and wood ducks are abundant, but great blue herons, bitterns, pied-billed grebes and rails may also be seen or heard. Tillman Road WMA is an excellent place to see a variety of songbirds throughout the spring, summer, and fall.

Many mammals, including deer, muskrats, beaver, mink and raccoons are found here as well. From May through July, it's not uncommon to see does with fawns. You're also likely to find salamanders and many other amphibians. In fact, one of the biggest attractions of this area is the potential to spot several species of frogs. The wildflowers attract a multitude of butterflies.

Route: The trail and elevated boardwalk start from the Wehrle Road parking area. The boardwalk runs about 300 hundred feet. Then, if you wish, step off and continue your walk on the loop trail. At approximately 0.25 mile you'll cross a foot bridge. Shortly, the trail bends right and circles back to the parking area.

Continue birdwatching on the other trails within Tillman Road Wildlife Management Area, if you wish. 3.5 miles of trails are available for exploration.

DEC issues yearly canoeing permits on a very limited basis to authorize canoeing and kayaking (strictly non-motorized) on the marsh and pond. Contact the NYS DEC, Buffalo office at (716) 851-7010 to apply for a permit.

Date:

Birds Seen:

Other Observations:

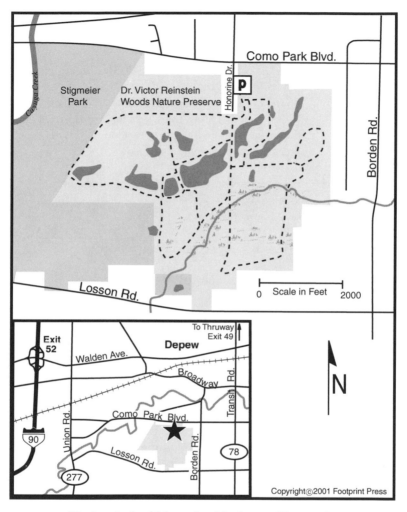

Reinstein Woods Nature Preserve

7

Reinstein Woods Nature Preserve — Trail

Location:	Cheektowaga, Erie County
Directions:	Take the NYS Thruway to exit 49. Head south on Route 78 then turn right (W) on Como Park Boulevard (or from Route 277 turn east on Como Park Boulevard). Turn south on Honorine Drive. Find the entrance and parking area in about 100 yards.
Admission:	Free (guided walks only - see below)
Trail Length:	0.25 mile
Time To Hike:	Approximately 30 minutes (or 60 minutes for the longer trail)
Trail Conditions:	Good, sometimes wet
Trail Surface:	Dirt
Trail Markings:	Reinstein Woods Nature Preserve markers
Trail Difficulty:	1
Birds Likely Seen:	Woodpeckers, nuthatches, chickadees, turkey vultures, shorebirds, hawks, herons, ducks and geese
Other Park Uses:	None
Contact:	NYS DEC, Region 9 270 Michigan Avenue, Buffalo, NY 14203 (716) 851-7201

Reinstein Woods Nature Preserve consists of approximately 300 acres of land surrounded by suburban development. The preserve is within the northern hardwood/beech-maple forest region, and includes mature forest, young forest, dense shrub thickets, and 19 ponds and marshes. Many species native to western New York, including the red-tailed hawk, pileated woodpecker, white-tailed deer, and great blue heron live within or visit the preserve and thrive under its protection. Native wildflowers, lichens, ferns, and fungi also abound in the preserve.

In the mid 1930s Dr. Victor Reinstein purchased the land as a private sanctuary. Between 1939 and 1960 ponds were created and 30,000 pine seedlings were planted. In 1986 DEC assumed ownership of the preserve.

Today, the Reinstein Woods Nature Preserve is managed to protect, preserve, perpetuate and enhance the area's natural resources, while offering environmental education opportunities. To fulfill these management objectives, DEC limits public access to **guided nature walks only**. DEC staff manage the reserve, oversee educational programs and arrange tours.

Call DEC at (716) 851-7201 to verify current tour dates and times. When you visit the preserve, meet your guide at the preserve parking lot.

Date:

Birds Seen:

Other Observations:

A hooded merganser in display.

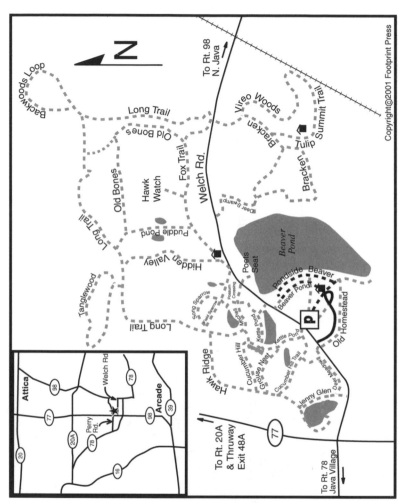

Beaver Meadow Audubon Center

8.

Beaver Meadow Audubon Center
— Pondside Trail & Beaver Pond Trail

Location:	North Java, Wyoming County
Directions:	Take the NYS Thruway to the Pembroke exit (48A). Head south on Route 77. At about 1.5 miles, before Java Center, turn left on Welch Road. Go about 0.25 mile to the flagpole parking area.
Admission:	Free (donations are accepted)
Trail Length:	About 0.25 mile
Time To Hike:	Approximately 20-30 minutes
Trail Conditions:	Well maintained, sometimes wet
Trail Surface:	Dirt trail
Trail Markings:	Wooden trail name signs
Trail Difficulty:	1
Birds Likely Seen:	Woodpeckers, nuthatches, chickadees, turkey vultures, hawks, warblers, tanagers, bluebirds, finches, shore birds, herons, grebes, ducks and geese
Other Park Uses:	Summer day camp, snowshoe rental, cross-country skiing, night activities, guided tours, astronomy and nature classes
Contact:	Buffalo Audubon Society Beaver Meadow Audubon Center 1610 Welch Road, North Java, NY 14113 (716) 457-3228

Nestled in west-central Wyoming County is the Beaver Meadow Audubon Center. The Buffalo Audubon Society sponsors, maintains and administers the center. Beaver Meadow is a 324-acre sanctuary with 8 miles of trails, all of which are excellent for birding. This includes the Jenny Glen Trail boardwalk, which is handicapped accessible.

Beaver Meadow is a must see if you're looking for a learning or education area dealing with nature and birds. It is set up primarily for nature appreciation and learning. Memberships are available and volunteers are appreciated. Some of the Audubon center activities include: maintaining a bluebird trail, summer day camp, family programs, nature classes, night walks, guided tours, cross-country ski tours, snowshoe rental, and astronomy classes.

The hands-on area in the visitor center is fun for people of all ages. It has a taxidermy display and a fine library. After a pleasing walk, go to the gift shop and snack bar, for a cooling or warming drink.

Route: Start the Pondside Trail from the visitor center. As you near the water, head left, and take advantage of the lookout platform. Notice how the plant and animal life coexists in the marsh. Continue walking and turn left to pick up Beaver Pond Trail and your return to the visitor center.

Other trails to try with particularly good birdwatching opportunities include:

Deer Meadow Trail—a woods trail that circles an open grass meadow. An interpretive sign assists with bird identification along the way.

Field Sparrow Trail—walk through the field and watch for sparrows.

Fox Trail—a mowed-grass path through a scrub field to a young arboretum. A spur trail leads to a hawk watch area.

Nuthatch Trail—a short walk through a pine forest with a bird observation area.

Date:

Birds Seen:

Other Observations:

Iroquois National Wildlife Refuge (NWR)

The Iroquois NWR covers about 10,000 acres and is one of over 500 National Wildlife Refuges administered by the US Fish and Wildlife Service, part of the Department of the Interior. Another refuge in New York State is Montezuma, near Syracuse. (See page 112.) The purpose of the refuge system is to manage wildlife and wildlife habitat.

Iroquois NWR was established in 1958 as the Oak Orchard National Wildlife Refuge under the authority of the Migratory Bird Conservation Act (Duck Stamp Act). In 1964 it was renamed Iroquois National Wildlife Refuge. It is bordered on two sides by state-managed wildlife areas. They are Tonawanda to the southwest and Oak Orchard to the east. These areas provide 9,000 additional acres of wildlife habitat.

The refuge has been identified as an "Important Bird Area" by the National Audubon Society. At least 266 species of birds use the refuge throughout the year. This is what draws approximately 100,000 human visitors to the area each year.

Canoeing and fishing are permitted in the refuge and hunters have great success in the fall. To protect nesting wildlife, all areas of the refuge except overlooks and nature trails, are closed to the public between March 1 and July 15. Three nature trails and the 4 overlooks are open daily, sunrise to sunset (unless otherwise posted.) Canoes or other nonmotorized boats are permitted between sunrise and sunset on Oak Orchard Creek, east of Route 63 only (check with the visitor center for access restrictions).

The visitor center (on Casey Road) office hours are Monday-Friday, year round (except holidays) from 7:30 AM - 4:00 PM. Also weekends from 9:00 AM - 5:00 PM during spring migration. Please stop in or call ahead for current information on rules, regulations, maps and permits.

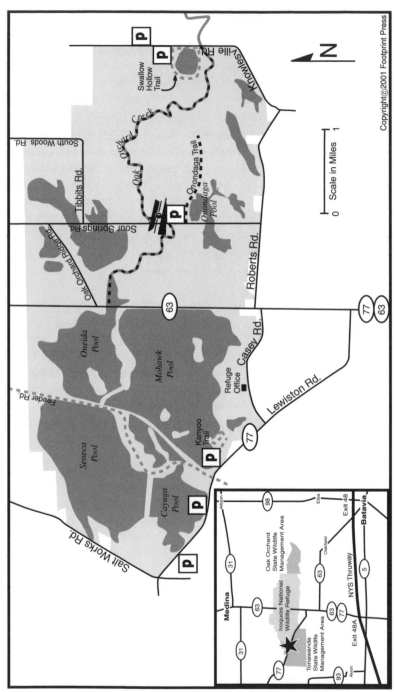

Iroquois National Wildlife Refuge

58

9.
Iroquois National Wildlife Refuge — Onondaga Trail

Location: Sour Springs Road, Alabama, Genesee County

Directions: Turn east from Route 63 on Oak Orchard Ridge Road. Then turn right (S) on Sour Springs Road. Cross Oak Orchard Creek and park at the Onondaga parking lot.

Admission: Free

Trail Length: 1 mile each way

Time To Hike: Approximately 1.5 hours

Trail Conditions: Sometimes wet

Trail Surface: Dirt and gravel

Trail Markings: Onondaga Trail sign

Trail Difficulty: 1

Birds Likely Seen: Woodpeckers, nuthatches, chickadees, thrushes, turkey vultures, grosbeaks, goldfinches, warblers, sparrows, herons, ducks and geese

Other Refuge Uses: Canoeing, fishing, trapping, hunting (regulations apply), snowshoeing, cross-country skiing and photography blinds (by permit and reservation only)

Contact: Iroquois National Wildlife Refuge
1101 Casey Road, Basom, NY 14013-9730
(716) 948-5445

Route: The trail leaves from the parking lot. When you reach the end, turn around and return.

Watch Onondaga Pool for ducks and geese as you walk. Don't be surprised to see deer along the trail. This trail is closed to nonhunters during gun deer hunting season.

Two other good birdwatching trails in Iroquois NWR are:
The Kanyoo Trail (a 1-mile loop and a 0.7-mile loop) at Mohawk Pool near Feeder Road and Lewiston Road, is open year-round, even during hunting season.
The Swallow Hollow Trail (a 1.4-mile loop) on Knowlesville Road near Oak Orchard Creek.

Date:

Birds Seen:

Other Observations:

10.

Iroquois National Wildlife Refuge
— Oak Orchard Creek Canoe Route

Location:	Sour Springs Road, Alabama, Genesee County
Directions:	Turn east from Route 63 on Oak Orchard Ridge Road. Then turn right (S) on Sour Springs Road for about 1.5 miles to Oak Orchard Creek. Limited parking is available on the sides of the road.
Admission:	Free
Route Length:	1 mile downstream to Route 63 or about 3 miles upstream to Knowlesville Road
Time To Canoe:	Approximately 1 hour to 4 hours or more
Water Conditions:	A narrow creek, sometimes low water level, fallen trees
Difficulty Level:	3
Birds Likely Seen:	Woodpeckers, nuthatches, chickadees, turkey vultures, herons, shorebirds, ducks and geese
Other Refuge Uses:	Hiking, fishing, trapping, hunting (regulations apply), snowshoeing, cross-country skiing and photography blinds (by permit and reservation only)
Contact:	Iroquois National Wildlife Refuge 1101 Casey Road, Basom, NY 14013-9730 (716) 948-5445

Only the creek waters of the refuge, between Route 63 and Knowlesville Road, are canoeable. This area is not a pleasure cruise. It often has logs and beaver dams across it, and many mosquitoes in the spring and summer. But, if you're looking for great opportunities to see wildlife, then this is the area to paddle.

Route: Starting from the Sour Springs Road creek crossing, you can head downstream (1 mile) to the Route 63 bridge or upstream (3 miles) to Knowlesville Road. (You can also launch from Knowlesville Road, if you prefer.) Watch for ducks, geese and even deer as you paddle. When you're ready, turn around and return to your launch area.

Date:

Birds Seen:

Other Observations:

Routes near Rochester

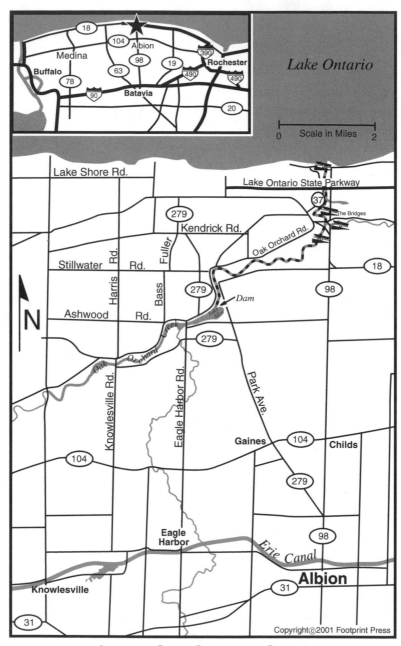

Lower Oak Orchard Creek

11.

Lower Oak Orchard Creek — Canoe Route

Location: Carlton, Orleans County

Directions: The creek is about 35 miles west of Rochester. Take Route 104 west to Route 98. Turn right and head north. A short distance after Route 98 and Route 18 merge, turn right at The Bridges area, and continue on Oak Orchard Road. Make a quick zigzag and turn left on County Road 37. Go north about 1 mile and the launch site (Orleans County Marine Park at Point Breeze) is ahead on the left. As an alternative, you could launch from The Bridges area. You might have to pay to launch, but it will make the route about a mile shorter.

Admission: Free

Route Distance: About 4 miles to the dam

Time To Canoe: Approximately 3 hours

Route Conditions: A wide, unobstructed stream

Difficulty Level: 1

Birds Likely Seen: Ducks, geese, shorebirds, herons, hawks, finches, warblers, woodpeckers and thrushes

Other Uses: Fishing, trapping

Contact: Orleans County
14016 Roue 31 West, Albion, NY 14411
(716) 589-7004

The northern section of Oak Orchard Creek which runs from the Waterport Hydropower dam to Lake Ontario provides the best birding opportunity on this creek. In the fall and spring, anglers fish near the hydro dam (currently Orion Power Company) for steelhead and salmon. Or, they head out into Lake Ontario and fish with downriggers.

In this section of Oak Orchard Creek you'll find plenty of restaurants, stores selling boating and fishing supplies, groceries, and fishing licenses. There are day use areas at Orleans County Park offering transient docking, picnic areas with grills, phone, restrooms, showers, and tourist information.

Route: If you start at the Orleans County Marine Park at Point Breeze launch (County Road 37) and head upstream (south) you'll have an easy return to your starting point. Much of the route is open so be sure to wear sunscreen. Don't forget your binoculars and camera, or fishing gear if that's your pleasure. Smallmouth bass, largemouth bass and pike are plentiful.

There are many small islands and sandbars where shorebirds and king-fishers like to feed. Waterfowl take advantage of these areas for breeding and migration. Also watch for birds of prey. You can approach the dam, but as you do, the water becomes shallow and swift.

Oak Orchard Creek can be broken into three sections, each providing different outdoor adventures. The northernmost section, described above is best for birding. Heading southwest (upstream), the next section runs from the Waterport hydropower dam to Route 104. The dam created a man-made reservoir (known locally as Lake Alice and labeled on some maps as Waterport Pond) which supports outdoor fun, including boating, water-skiing and fishing.

Continuing southwest (upstream), the section from Route 104 to Medina includes some fast water excitement for rafting, kayaking and canoeing.

A southern area of Oak Orchard Creek is included in the Iroquois National Wildlife Refuge segment (see page 57).

Date:

Birds Seen:

Other Observations:

Braddock Bay

Braddock Bay is the place to be if you're trying to see birds of prey—as many as 100,000 in the spring. The waters of Lake Ontario are cold in the spring and don't create warm thermals. Birds rely on the thermals to assist their flight so Lake Ontario is too wide and cold for them to cross. Instead, the birds go around Lake Ontario where they can find the thermals they need. The shoreline at Braddock Bay turns toward the southeast. Therefore on days with good southwest winds, migrating birds concentrate at this point.

The Braddock Bay Raptor Research area is on the north side of Manitou Beach Road, adjacent to the bay. In 1984, a hawk banding station was built, and is open to the public. Volunteers catch birds in nets and band their legs with a numbered metal band. This allows them to count bird species and track

The hawk banding station at Braddock Bay Raptor Research

migration patterns. The trail is open year-round, but in late April they offer an annual event of walks, talks and demonstrations.

Braddock Bay Park is on the east side of the bay. Here you can see the bird of prey migration from a large lookout platform. In the spring volunteers count the number of raptors flying overhead. Also, from the park, you can walk the trail to Cranberry Pond—another great birding location.

Braddock Bay has excellent waterfowl hunting and fishing, including ice fishing in winter. Numerous creeks empty into the bay, with Salmon Creek being the biggest. Birding and fishing from a canoe or boat is a lot of fun. At times the outlet into Lake Ontario can get a bit rough, so it's not recommended that anyone take a canoe into this area. Even with a larger boat, you may hit bottom or shear a prop if you don't navigate the channel properly. You can access Braddock Bay from launches at Braddock Bait & Tackle (which includes a restaurant) on the west or Braddock Bay Marina on the east. There is a charge for launching boats at the marinas.

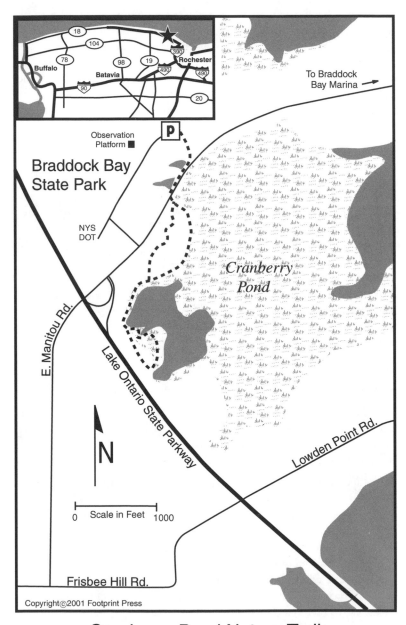

Cranberry Pond Nature Trail

12.
Cranberry Pond Nature Trail

Location:	East Manitou Road, Greece, Monroe County
Directions:	Exit from Lake Ontario State Parkway on East Manitou Road. Go north and turn left into Braddock Bay Park (going straight takes you to Braddock Bay Marina). Turn right at the "T." Pass the observation platform on your left and continue straight to the big parking area.
Admission:	Free
Trail Length:	About 1.5 miles
Time To Hike:	Approximately 60 minutes
Trail Conditions:	Maintained, but wet at times
Trail Surface:	Dirt and grass path
Trail Markings:	Trail is marked with number signs
Difficulty Level:	1
Birds Likely Seen:	Buteo and accipiter hawks, bald eagles, turkey vultures, ducks, geese, coots, shorebirds, swans, redwing blackbirds, herons, bitterns, warblers, owls, chickadees, nuthatches, titmice and brown creepers
Other Park Uses:	Fishing, picnicking and boating
Contact:	Town of Greece Parks and Recreation 500 Maiden Lane, Greece, NY 14616 (716) 663-0200

Route: The trail starts from the east side of the parking lot. Pass carved wooden figures as you start the trail, then follow the trail to East Manitou Road. Turn right and head south for a short distance. When you get near the curve in the road, carefully cross the road and re-enter the trail at the marker. Zigzag through the thicket, and watch for warblers, chickadees, titmice and nuthatches until you get to the opening with Cranberry Pond on your left. Usually there are mallards, teals and woodies in the potholes. You can stop here and return to the parking lot, or you can continue around part of the pond and enter the woods. While you're in this wooded area, watch for owls and woodland birds. When you get back to where the open area meets the trees, you can go back the way you came or proceed to the left and follow the road back.

Date:

Birds Seen:

Other Observations:

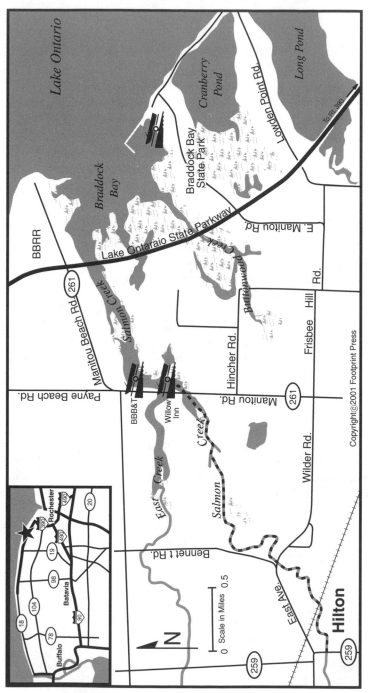

Salmon Creek - Canoe Route

13.

Salmon Creek — Canoe Route

Location:	Manitou Road, Greece, Monroe County
Directions:	From Lake Ontario State Parkway, exit at Manitou Beach Road and head south to the entrance of Braddock Bay Bait & Tackle or, continue to the parking area near the Willow Inn(less boat traffic). Or, from Route 104, turn north on Manitou Road (Route 261) and head north to the boat launch.
Admission:	Free launch for canoes from Willow Inn
Route Length:	About 1 to 5 miles
Time to Canoe:	1 hour to all day
Water Conditions:	Occasionally shallow
Difficulty Level:	1, 2 (sometimes whitecaps on open water)
Birds Likely Seen:	Buteo and accipiter hawks, bald eagles, turkey vultures, ducks, geese, swans, teals, coots, shorebirds, redwing blackbirds, herons, bitterns, warblers, owls, chickadees and nuthatches
Other Uses:	Fishing, hunting and nature photography
Contact:	Town of Greece Parks and Recreation 500 Maiden Lane, Greece, NY 14616 (716) 663-0200

Route: After putting in you can go to the left toward Braddock Bay and Lake Ontario or, as I prefer, turn right, go under the bridge and head into the Salmon Creek area. From here you can easily paddle all the way to the town of Hilton and beyond.

Watch for shorebirds, ducks, geese, bitterns and herons, and keep your eyes to the sky for raptors. This area has some of the best birding in Western New York.

Date:

Birds Seen:

Other Observations:

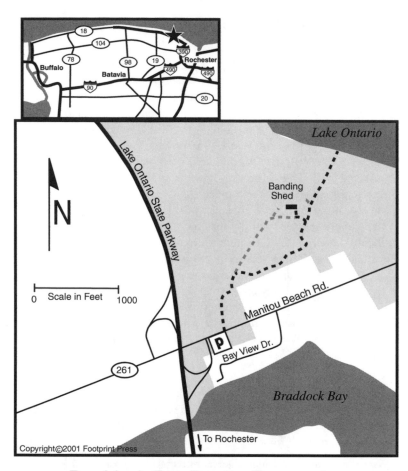

Braddock Bay Raptor Research

14.
Braddock Bay Raptor Research — Waterfowl Refuge Trail

Location:	Manitou Beach Road, Hilton, Monroe County
Directions:	Exit from Lake Ontario State Parkway on Manitou Beach Road. Park in the lot on the south side of Manitou Beach Road, next to the Lake Ontario State Parkway.
Admission:	Free
Trail Length:	0.9-mile round trip
Time To Hike:	30 Minutes
Trail Conditions:	Easy-to-follow, well maintained trail
Trail Surface:	Dirt and grass path and boardwalk
Trail Markings:	None
Difficulty Level:	1
Birds Likely Seen:	Buteo and accipiter hawks, eagles, owls, ducks, geese, turkey vultures, warblers, bluebirds, goldfinches and typical woodland birds
Other Uses:	Photography
Contact:	Braddock Bay Raptor Research 432 Manitou Beach Road, Hilton, NY 14468 (716) 392-5685
	NYS DEC, Region 8 6274 Avon-Lima Road, Avon, NY 14414 (716) 226-2466

Route: From the parking lot, carefully cross Manitou Beach Road. At the start of the trail you may see bluebirds and goldfinches. Head north and take the trail into the spruce and pines. Follow the main trail across the wooden boardwalk adjacent to private property. Continue straight and follow the signs to the raptor banding station. Watch for warblers. As you come to the banding station, turn left and be sure to obey the rules posted next to the wooden walkway.

Please do not wander around the blind. There are numerous trap wires tied into the banding station. The wires are linked to baited nets. A person in the blind pulls the wire to trap the bird when a bird comes to the net. Stay on the trails and be quiet, especially in the spring so you don't interfere with the trapping and banding of birds. This is a research area, and we must respect what is taking place.

At this point you can return the way you came. Or, go to the lake by returning to the trail and turning left (instead of right). Then continue straight, without any turns, and go through the woods another 0.1 mile to the lakeshore edge. Here you may find shore birds, brants, geese, swans and many diving ducks. Sometimes they're close, other times good optics or binoculars are needed. To return, reverse your direction and go back to your starting point.

If you time it right (February through April, with the end of March as the peak), you should see many long-eared and saw whet owls resting in the conifers during the day.

Date:

Birds Seen:

Other Observations:

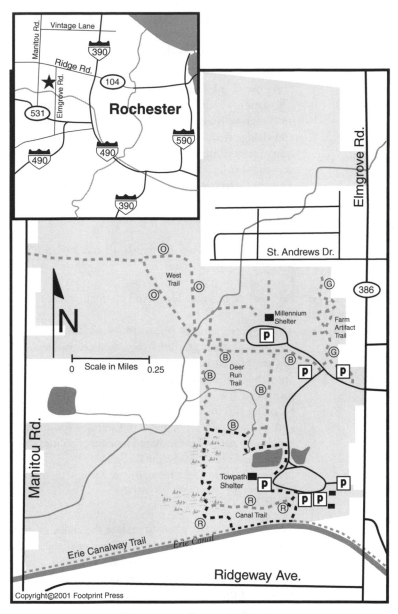

Greece Canal Park

15.
Greece Canal Park — Trail

Location:	Elmgrove Road, Greece, Monroe County
Directions:	The park is about 0.25 mile north of the canal bridge on Elmgrove Road or about 1 mile south of Route 104 (Ridge Road). The park entrance is located on the west side of Elmgrove Road. After entering the park, take the first left. Straight leads to the field sports area. This trail starts at the Towpath Shelter parking lot.
Admission:	Free
Trail Length:	Approximately 1.5 miles
Time to Hike:	About 60 minutes
Trail Conditions:	Trail goes through woods, grasslands and lowlands which are sometimes wet
Trail Surface:	Dirt and grass path
Trail Markings:	Red, yellow and blue blazes and plastic markers
Difficulty Level:	1, 2
Birds Likely Seen:	Ducks, geese, turkeys, pheasants, woodpeckers, thrushes, chickadees, nuthatches, titmice, warblers, finches, bluebirds, wrens and sparrows
Other Park Uses:	Snowshoeing, cross-country skiing, field sports, picnicking (has shelters), tennis, horseback riding, bicycling and in-line skating (allowed on park roads and on canal path), boating, canoeing and fishing in canal. The park does not have launching facilities, but there is a platform at the canal edge.
Contact:	Monroe County Parks Department. 171 Reservoir Avenue, Rochester, NY 14620 (716) 256-4950

In 2001, Monroe County Parks has plans to reblaze the trails, creating loops that are color coded. While, long-term this will be beneficial, in the short-term it creates some complexity. The colors listed in the following route and on the map are the new blaze colors. If you encounter other colors, they may be remnants of the old color scheme.

The first leg of this route has a variety of woodland birds such as chickadees, titmice, nuthatches and woodpeckers. Further in you'll find woodland and hedgerow-loving birds, such as chickadees, wrens and warblers. The field area has lowland and grass loving birds, such as bluebirds and swallows during the spring and summer. You might also see deer, fox, woodchucks and other mammals. These trails provide a good combination of habitats for birds and other animals.

Route: From the Towpath Shelter parking area, head north along the roadway, passing a pond. When you get to the woods, turn left onto an unmarked trail (used to be red) and enter the woods. Continue straight on the blue trail (don't take the trail to the right) for about 0.1 mile and cross the creek. Continue for another 0.1 mile until the blue trail takes a sharp right. Turn left on an unmarked trail and head south for about 0.25 mile until you see the red marker. To end the hike sooner, turn left and return to the Towpath Shelter area.

For a longer hike, bear right on the red trail (used to be blue). Head across the field, climb the bank to the Erie Canal and turn left (E) onto the Erie Canalway Trail. Continue until you get to the "Greece Canal Park" sign. Turn left and proceed down the steps to the road. The Towpath Shelter parking area will be to your left.

Date:

Birds Seen:

Other Observations:

Even without binoculars, you can enjoy a scene like this.
A mourning dove and her two babies rest on a rock beside the trail.

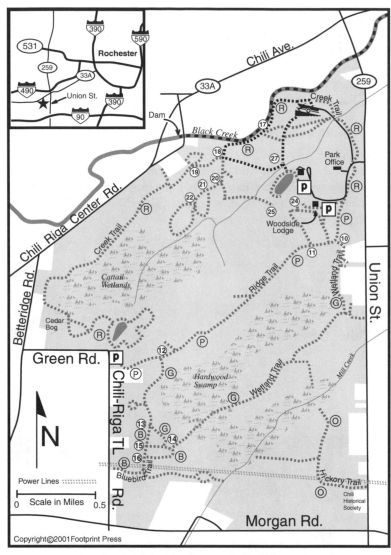

Black Creek Park

16.
Black Creek Park — Trail

Location:	Route 259 (Union Street), Chili, Monroe County
Directions:	The entrance is about 0.7 mile south of Route 490 on Route 259. The park office building is in front of you as you enter. Turn right and drive to the north end of the park. Limited parking is available. The creek is down a hill in front of you.
Admission:	Free
Trail Length:	About 2 miles
Time To Hike:	60 minutes
Trail Conditions:	Trails are well maintained
Trail Surface:	Dirt and grass path
Trail Markings:	Junctions have blue and white numbered signs and trails are color blazed
Difficulty Level:	1
Birds Likely Seen:	Mallards, wood ducks, teals, geese, hawks, herons, orioles, bluebirds, finches, warblers, wrens and swallows
Other Park Uses:	Snowshoeing, cross-country skiing, model airplane flying, fishing, canoeing, horseback riding, picnicking
Contact:	Monroe County Parks Department 171 Reservoir Avenue, Rochester, NY 14620 (716) 256-4950

Black Creek Park has many trails that are great for birdwatching, and all are worth hiking. The route described below has a blend of habitats so birdwatching and other nature observations are greatly enhanced.

Route: Take the path downhill toward the creek, and veer left keeping the creek to your right. Watch for finches as you cross the grassy picnic area. There is a slight rise as the trail parallels the creek. Look down to your right and see if you can spot any ducks in the creek. Eventually, the trail will veer to the left, leaving the creek. Continue to the junction with marker 18 and turn left. (Veering right puts you on a longer, outer trail. Straight takes you toward the marsh area). As you walk along the brushy field, watch for the buteo (soaring) hawks.

At junction 27, turn right and cross the wooden bridge. As you peer across the pond, watch for birds and occasional deer drinking from the pond.

Turn around, cross the same bridge, then turn right. Staying to the left side of the field, head across toward the wooded hedgerow. Along this area you should see bluebirds near their boxes. Cross through the narrow hedgerow, turn right and follow the path toward the metal gate where you parked.

Date:

Birds Seen:

Other Observations:

17.

Black Creek Park — Canoe Route

Location: Route 259 (Union Street), Chili, Monroe County

Directions: The entrance is about 0.7 mile south of Route 490 on Route 259. The park office building is in front of you as you enter. Turn right and drive to the north end of the park. Limited parking is available. The creek is down a hill in front of you.

Admission: Free

Route Length: 1.5 miles upstream to a dam and back

Time To Canoe: 60 minutes

Water Conditions: Normally a placid creek, but use caution during times of heavy rain or spring runoff

Difficulty Level: 1, 2

Birds Likely Seen: Mallards, wood ducks, teals, kingfishers, cedar waxwings and swallows

Other Park Uses: Snowshoeing, cross-country skiing, model airplane flying, fishing, hiking, horseback riding, and picnicking

Contact: Monroe County Parks Department
171 Reservoir Avenue, Rochester, NY 14620
(716) 256-4950

Route: Take the path downhill to launch your canoe or kayak. (Monroe County Parks Department plans to build a launching structure in 2001.) When the water is high, swift, or during spring runoff, you should be careful of submerged objects in the creek. You have a choice of going upstream to the left, or downstream to the right. Heading upstream is usually easy paddling. Watch for kingfishers diving into the water or cedar waxwings catching insects in the air. Also watch for blue-wing teal, mallards and other water birds in this riparian (water edge) habitat. If you enjoy fishing, toss small bait with an ultra light pole, or in parts of the creek use a fly rod to catch bass and pike.

Upstream, at about 0.75 mile, you'll come to an old dam. The homeowners discourage trespassing, so stay in your canoe, paddle back downstream and take out where you entered, or con-

Mallard ducks paddle the waters.

79

tinue downstream. From this spot you can paddle a fair distance, about 6.5 miles to the Genesee River. As you continue, the creek flows into more populated areas where birds and wildlife become less frequent. Make sure you plan ahead where and how you will take your canoe out. One possible downstream spot to take out is Scottsville-Chili Road (Route 386).

Date:

Birds Seen:

Other Observations:

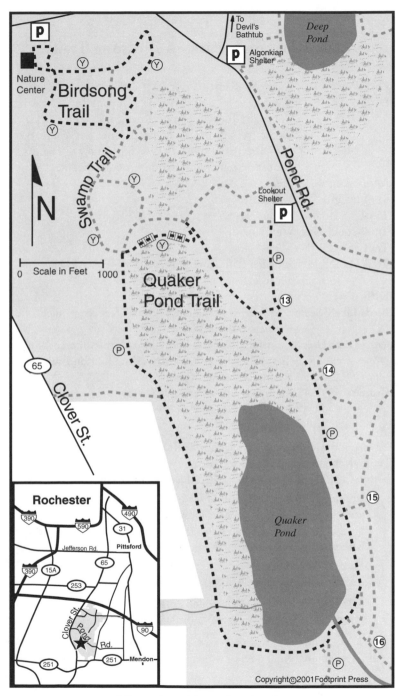

Mendon Ponds Park

18.
Mendon Ponds Park — Birdsong Trail

Location: Route 65 (Clover Street), Mendon, Monroe County

Directions: The park is located on Route 65 about 2 miles south of Route 253 (Lehigh Station Road). It has three entrances on the east side of Clover Street. They are well marked with directional signs. In this case, follow the signs to the nature center at the southernmost entrance.

Admission: Free

Trail Length: 1.1-mile loop

Time To Hike: 30 minutes

Trail Conditions: Wide lane

Trail Surface: Mainly grass

Trail Markings: Wooden trail name signs, yellow blazes are being added in 2001

Difficulty: 1

Birds Likely Seen: Chickadees, nuthatches, brown creepers, titmice, warblers and finches

Other Park Uses: Canoeing, hiking, biking (on park roads), picnicking (has shelters), cross-country skiing (not on Birdsong or Swamp Trails) and fishing

Contact: Monroe County Parks Department
171 Reservoir Avenue, Rochester, NY 14620
(716) 256-4950

During the last ice age a glacier a mile thick that went as far south as the Pennsylvania border covered this area. Mendon Ponds Park is a National Natural Landmark because of its glacial landforms such as:

Kettles - When a large piece of ice breaks off from a glacier, the water from the glacier deposits gravel and debris around the large block. Then the block melts and leaves a big hole in the ground filled with water. Devil's Bathtub is a good example of this.

Kames - When rivers flow on top of a glacier they spill over and deposit soil into big piles.

Eskers - When a river flows under a glacier it deposits material in the tunnel beds. When the ice melts a ridge of the deposits remain.

Mendon Ponds Park was dedicated in 1928 and has about 30 miles of trails. The nature center offers a wide range of exhibits and programs.

Birdsong Trail is well known for the chickadees that eat sunflower seeds from your hand. Even the nuthatches have learned this trick. Stand still with seeds in your palm, and hand raised. You can get seed from the nature center, or bring your own.

Take sunflower seeds to feed the black-capped chickadees.

Route: The trail starts at the trellis near the nature center. From the trellis, bear left, then turn right at the first junction. Follow the Birdsong Trail markers for a 1.1-mile loop, or include the Swamp Trail and Quaker Pond Trail for a longer adventure.

Date:

Birds Seen:

Other Observations:

19.

Mendon Ponds Park — Quaker Pond Trail

Location: Route 65 (Clover Street), Mendon, Monroe County

Directions: The park is located on Route 65 about 2 miles south of Route 253 (Lehigh Station Road). Turn left (E) at the third park entrance on Pond Road. Pass the nature center and Algonkian Shelter. Park at the Lookout Shelter parking area.

Admission: Free

Trail Length: 2.5-mile loop

Time To Hike: Approximately 90 minutes

Trail Conditions: Well maintained trail

Trail Surface: Mainly grass path

Trail Markings: Wooden trail name signs, purple blazes are being added in 2001

Difficulty: 1

Birds Likely Seen: Chickadees, bluebirds, ducks, geese, nuthatches, rails, herons, bitterns, tree swallows, bobolinks, meadowlarks, hawks, turkeys, titmice, warblers, finches and shorebirds

Other Park Uses: Canoeing (although not on Quaker Pond), hiking, biking (on park roads), picnicking (has shelters), cross-country skiing and fishing

Contact: Monroe County Parks Department
171 Reservoir Avenue, Rochester, NY 14620
(716) 256-4950

Route: Head west from the parking area then turn left. At junction 13, bear right, then right again on the Quaker Pond Trail. Take the next left on the boardwalk, then continue bearing left around Quaker Pond. Water will be visible only at the southern end.

As you circle Quaker Pond, look for the beaver houses and watch the waterfowl in the pond. In spring and fall, ponds like this are places for waterfowl to rest before continuing on their migration. (Unfortunately, many people feed waterfowl, which makes them less likely to migrate.) At dusk or dawn you might be lucky enough to see deer.

Take sunflower seeds to feed the black-capped chickadees from your hand. They'll circle your head looking for a handout.

Date:

Birds Seen:

Other Observations:

Routes in the
Finger Lakes Region

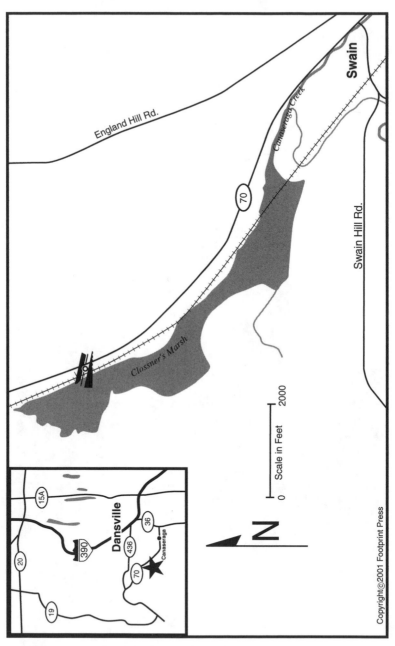

Clossner's Marsh (Canaseraga Creek)

20.
Clossner's Marsh — Canoe Route

Location: Headwaters of Canaseraga Creek, Swain, Allegany County

Directions: Take I-390 to Dansville (exit 4) and turn right on Route 36. Head south and turn right on Route 70. Continue through Canaseraga, Garwoods and Swain. The parking area is on the left (south side) about 2 miles past Swain, next to the railroad.

Admission: Free

Route Distance: 1 mile (more if you choose to explore)

Time To Canoe: 1 hour to all day

Water Conditions: Calm open water in a marsh

Difficulty Level: 1

Birds Likely Seen: Shorebirds, bitterns, herons, woodpeckers, finches, blackbirds, warblers, bluebirds, geese, widgeons, mallards, wood ducks, blue-wing and green-wing teals and, gadwals on occasion

Other Uses: Fishing, trapping, photography and hunting

Contact: NYS DEC, Region 8
6274 East Avon-Lima Road, Avon, NY 14414
(716) 226-2466

This watershed is known locally as Clossner's Marsh. It is the headwaters of Canaseraga Creek.

Route: Go to the far right of the parking lot, down the path to launch your canoe. Duck under the railroad bridge to access the marsh. Paddle anywhere you wish.

Keep your binoculars and camera focused on the marsh edges as you paddle. In this habitat, there are great opportunities to see shore birds, herons, swans, geese, ducks, turkey vultures, hawks and, possibly osprey. One day while scouting the area I saw an osprey diving into the water. In the spring, people come here to fish for bullhead.

Date:

Birds Seen:

Other Observations:

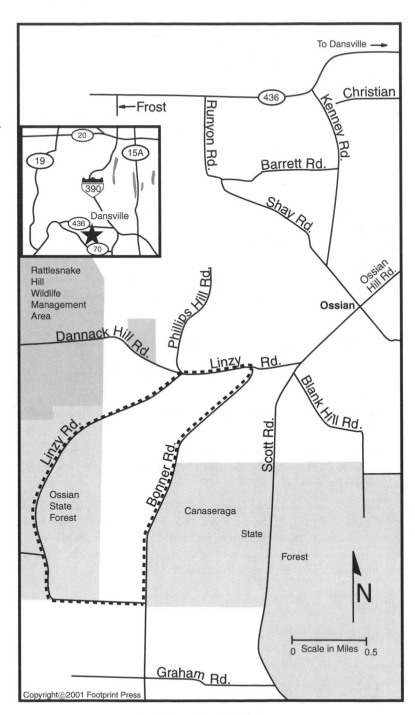

Ossian State Forest

21.
Ossian State Forest
— Bicycle or Driving Loop

Location: Towns of Grove, Nunda, and Burns, Livingston and Allegany Counties

Directions: Take I-390 to Dansville (exit 5). Go under the bridge and turn right on Route 36. At the "T" intersection, turn right (W) on Route 436. Turn left (S) after crossing Canaseraga Creek on Ossian Hill Road. Go about 4 miles through the town of Ossian. Continue straight as the road turns into Linzy Road. Turn left on Bonner Road and the beginning of the loop.

Admission: Free

Route Distance: About 5 miles

Time To Drive Route: About 30 minutes by car (longer if you wish)

Route Conditions: Dirt road

Route Markings: Road signs and NY State Forest markers

Difficulty Level: 1 if driving, 3 if bicycling

Birds Likely Seen: Hawks, finches, bluebirds, orioles, warblers, woodpeckers, nuthatches, chickadees, titmice, tanagers, waterfowl and thrushes

Other Uses: Fishing, hunting, trapping, snowshoeing, horseback riding, cross-country skiing and nature study

Contact: NYS DEC, Region 8
6274 East Avon-Lima Road, Avon, NY 14414
(716) 226-2466

Ossian State Forest is a tract of land which adjoins the 5,100-acre Rattlesnake Hill Wildlife Management Area. Rattlesnake Hill was purchased in the 1930s under the Federal Resettlement Administration and is one of many that were turned over to the DEC for development as a wildlife management area. The area is a blend of mature woodland, fields, open meadows, old growth orchards and conifer plantations. It is appropriately named. Timber rattlesnakes, once prevalent in the region, are now occasionally found in remote spots.

There are a few small, man-made marshes that provide limited waterfowl hunting and places for beaver, mink, deer and raccoon to thrive. Some of the deeper waters are stocked annually with trout. Portions of Canaseraga Creek, Hovey Brook and Sugar Creek which run through this region, are known trout waters.

To see birds and other wild creatures from this route, you don't even have to leave your car. Or, for a closer encounter, try bicycling the route. Either way, there are places where you can stop and walk, especially around the small ponds.

Route: Start the loop at Bonner Road heading south. During the summer, bluebirds and goldfinches can be seen in the fields and hedgerows as you head up the hill. Continue about 1.9 miles and turn right on the dirt road. At 2.4 miles a small pond will be on your right. Many people camp, fish, and hike in this area. As you continue, watch for turkey and the variety of woodpeckers that frequent the area. I have also seen deer drinking from the small beaver pond on your right.

As you start coming down the hill, watch for hawks, and check out the beaver ponds on your left. When you get to Linzy Road, turn right and continue back to the four corners.

Or, turn left on Dannack Hill Road and Ebert Road if you want to explore Rattlesnake Hill.

Date:

Birds Seen:

Other Observations:

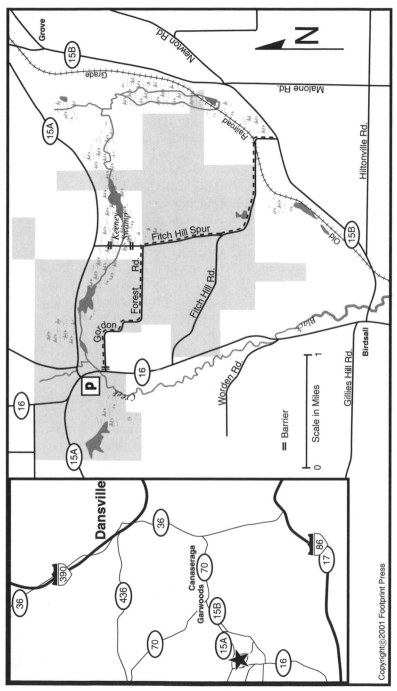

Keeney Swamp State Forest

22.

Keeney Swamp State Forest
— Bicycle or Driving Route

Location: Birdsall, Allegany County
Directions: From I-390 take exit 4 (Dansville) and turn right on Route 36. Head south and turn right on Route 70. Continue through the town of Canaseraga. Turn left at the village of Garwoods. Take County Road 15B about 1 mile then turn right on County Road 15A. Continue about 3 miles and turn left on County Road 16. In a few hundred yards turn left (yellow metal gate) on the state forest dirt road near the creek. This is Gordon Forest Road and the start of your route. (There is a parking lot at intersection of County Roads 15A and 16.)
Admission: Free
Route Distance: About 3.5 miles (more if you choose to explore)
Time to Drive: About 30 minutes by car (longer if you wish)
Route Conditions: The dirt road is sometimes muddy (gates are often closed during winter and at other times depending on road conditions)
Difficulty Level: 1 if driving, 2 if bicycling
Birds Likely Seen: Woodland birds, finches, warblers, bluebirds, herons, shore birds, blackbirds, geese, widgeons, mallards, blue-wing and green-wing teal and wood ducks
Other Uses: Trapping, canoeing, fishing, hunting and photography
Contact: NYS DEC, Region 9
5425 County Route 48, Belmont, NY 14813
(716) 268-5392

Route: Start into Keeney Swamp State Forest at the yellow metal gate and head east about 0.4 mile. The road will zigzag to the south another 0.4 mile mile, and then head east again, for 0.6 mile. Then the road will come to a "T." Going left takes you to the marsh, which is officially part of Keeney Swamp Wildlife Area. In this habitat, there are opportunities to see shore birds, herons, swans, geese, ducks, turkey vultures and hawks.

If you go to the right the route continues another 2 miles to the finish. At about 0.8 mile, Fitch Hill Road will come in from the right. Continue another 0.2 mile and the road turns left. Check the water area on your left for birds. At the end, turn left on County Road 15B to return to Garwoods and Route 70.

Although much of Keeney Swamp can be canoed, it is shallow, and in some spots, very confined. A kayak would work better.

Date:

Birds Seen:

Other Observations:

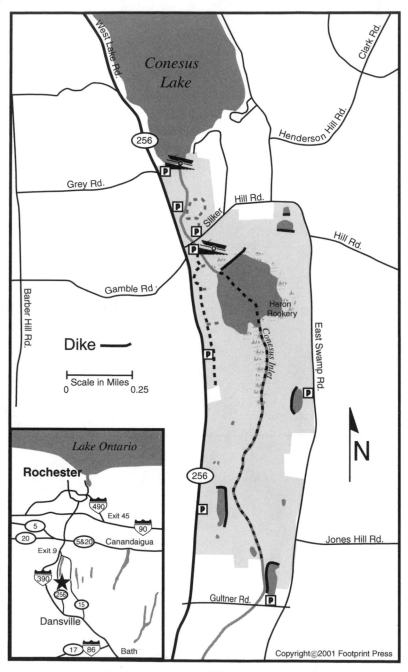

Conesus Fish and Wildlife Management Area

23.

Conesus Inlet Fish and Wildlife Management Area — Trail

Location:	South end of Conesus Lake, Livingston County
Directions:	Take I-390 to Route 15 (Conesus Lake exit). Then head south on Route 15 to Route 256. Head south on Route 256 past the lake about 0.5 mile to Sliker Hill Road. Turn left on Sliker Hill Road. Park at the state access parking lot immediately on the right. There is another parking area further down Sliker Hill Road, on the east side of Conesus Inlet.
Admission:	Free
Trail Distance:	About 1 mile each way
Time To Hike:	Approximately 60 minutes
Trail Conditions:	Dirt and mowed-grass path
Trail Markings:	Trail signs
Difficulty Level:	1
Birds Likely Seen:	Variety of ducks, variety of geese, numerous shore birds, herons, hawks, goldfinches, bluebirds, variety of warblers, woodpeckers, nuthatches, chickadees, wrens, titmice, blackbirds, sparrows and thrushes
Other Uses:	Fishing, hunting, snowshoeing and cross-country skiing (swimming is not allowed)
Contact:	NYS DEC, Region 8 6274 East Avon-Lima Road, Avon, NY 14414 (716) 226-2466

Conesus Lake is a very popular and heavily used lake that supports a cottage community. There is a lot of activity on the lake and immediate waterfront year-round.

The Conesus Inlet Fish and Wildlife Management Area is a marsh at the south end of the lake that covers over 1,168 acres. DEC, which subsequently initiated wildlife programs to conserve and protect this vital wetland resource, purchased the land in the late 1960s. In 1979 an additional 83 acres were added to provide boat access to the lake, and preserve critical pike spawning habitat. The latest purchase was 48 acres in 2001.

In the late winter and early spring you can see walleye gathering in the shallows near the main dike. It is not uncommon to see fish in the 10-pound range.

The trail along the west side of the marsh has three observation platforms which make perfect bird viewing spots.

Route: From the parking lot, head south for about 0.1 mile to the first observation platform. Keep your binoculars or spotting scope and camera ready. This area has abundant birds and other wildlife.

Continue on the trail, and stop at each platform to look for shorebirds, ducks and perhaps a glimpse at bitterns. At the end of the trail, turn around and reverse direction.

Dikes around small ponds are accessible from three additional parking areas (further south on Route 256, on Gultner Road, and on East Swamp Road). They make good vantage points for viewing birds but the grasses on them may not be mowed.

Date:

Birds Seen:

Other Observations:

24.
Conesus Inlet Fish and Wildlife Management Area — Canoe Route

Location:	South end of Conesus Lake, Livingston County
Directions:	Take I-390 to Route 15 (Conesus Lake exit). Then head south on Route 15 to Route 256. Head south on Route 256 past the lake about 0.5 mile to Sliker Hill Road. Turn left on Sliker Hill Road. Park at the state access parking lot immediately on the right.
Admission:	Free
Route Distance:	About 2 miles round trip
Time To Canoe:	Approximately 90 minutes
Route Conditions:	Open water surrounded by marsh. Late in the summer it gets harder to paddle because of thickening vegetation.
Difficulty Level:	1, 2
Birds Likely Seen:	Variety of ducks, variety of geese, numerous shore birds, herons, hawks, goldfinches, bluebirds, variety of warblers, woodpeckers, nuthatches, chickadees, titmice blackbirds, sparrows and thrushes.
Other Uses:	Fishing, hunting, snowshoeing and cross-country skiing (swimming is not allowed)
Contact:	NYS DEC, Region 8 6274 East Avon-Lima Road, Avon, NY 14414 (716) 226-2466

The Conesus Inlet is a waterway that winds through a marsh and drains water from the surrounding hills into Conesus Lake. Start the route from the parking lot by carrying your canoe or kayak (100 yards) to the dike to launch. Motors, including electric motors, are not allowed. This is shallow water, so when the water is low or the weeds get high you may have to pole through some of the marsh.

By canoeing the inlet, you can get close to wildlife, including the great blue heron rookery at the southeast end of the marsh. Look for a cluster of large nests high in the trees. Please do not disturb the rookery, especially in spring. The wildlife is abundant wherever you choose to paddle. This is a good place for close-up photography. Watch for shorebirds, ducks, geese, and bitterns and, of course, the herons.

Date:

Birds Seen:

Other Observations:

Hemlock Lake & Canadice Lake Watershed

A critical portion of the Hemlock and Canadice Lake watershed is owned, managed and controlled by the city of Rochester. The city owns all property adjacent to the shores of these lakes. The entirely undeveloped shorelines are unique among all the Finger Lakes, often evoking comparison to the Adirondacks. Both lakes are drinking water supply reservoirs for parts of Monroe County.

The watershed has been designated as part of New York State's Important Bird Area (IBA) program. These watersheds meet a number of IBA criteria including:

- Support an exceptional diversity of bird species
- Contain habitat that is rare, threatened or unusual
- Exceptionally representative of natural or near-natural habitat
- Support long-term research and/or monitoring

Brochures describing the IBA are available at the kiosk at the north end of Hemlock Lake.

These two Finger Lakes offer a pristine environment for nature observation and birdwatching. There are no cottages or docks along the shorelines.

Boating is allowed on the lakes but maximum size allowed is 16 feet (17 feet for canoes). Motors must be a maximum of 10 horsepower. You can find people fishing these waters year-round.

Canadice has an excellent trail running along the west side where there are many snags for cavity-nesting birds. It's common to see deer and turkey along this trail as well. During migration, you may spot loons along with many other species of waterfowl in the open water on both lakes. The south end of Hemlock Lake is the best area for possible sightings of bald eagles. This area is used for New York State's eagle and osprey reintroduction programs.

A free, annual permit is required for any activity in or on these watershed areas. Pick up a permit at a kiosk at the north end of Hemlock Lake Park, send a stamped self-addressed envelope to City of Rochester Watershed Permit, 7412 Rix-Hill Road, Hemlock, NY 14466 (716) 367-3160, or, download a copy at www.ci.rochester.ny.us/watershedpermit.htm. Please read and follow all regulations on the permit.

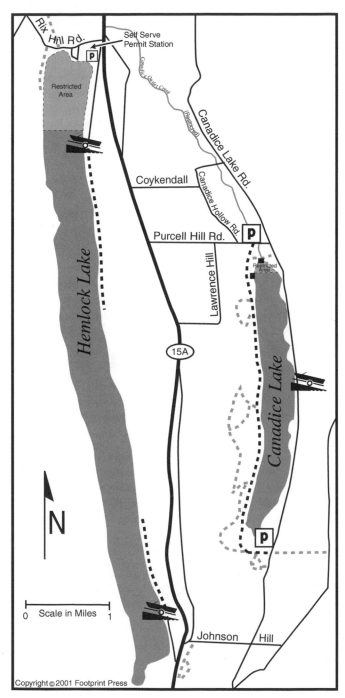

Canadice and Hemlock Lakes

25.
Hemlock Lake — Trail

Location:	Hemlock Lake, Livingston and Ontario Counties
Directions:	From Rochester, head south on Route 15A through the town of Hemlock. In about a mile turn right onto Rix Hill Road for the northern parking area. Or, continue south on 15A for another 7 miles to the southern access road.
Admission:	Free (permit required)
Trail Length:	North trail is 1.5 miles each way
	South trail is 1.25 miles each way
Time To Hike:	About 3 hours (longer if you wish)
Trail Conditions:	Dirt and grass path
Trail Markings:	"Hemlock Canadice Watershed" signs
Difficulty Level:	1
Birds Likely Seen:	Variety of ducks, variety of geese, numerous shore birds, herons, eagles, hawks, finches, bluebirds, variety of warblers, tanagers, woodpeckers, nuthatches, titmice, chickadees, and thrushes
Other Uses:	Restricted small craft boating, fishing, hunting snowshoeing and cross-country skiing (swimming is not allowed)
Contact:	City of Rochester
	7412 Rix-Hill Road, Hemlock, NY 14466
	(716) 367-3160

Hemlock Lake has two trails on the east side of the lake. One starts and finishes at the north end, and runs for 1.5 miles. The other trail starts and finishes at the south end and is 1.25 miles long.

The southern area tends to be better for birdwatching. As far back as the early 1970s, it was the site of the only bald eagle nest in the entire state; an indicator of the high quality, long-term stewardship of this land by the City of Rochester.

There are also a couple of small trails at the north end of the lake, off Rix-Hill Road and on the west side of the lake off Mission Road (see permit map) that are good for woodland birds and tanagers.

Date:

Birds Seen:

Other Observations:

26.
Hemlock Lake — Canoe Route

Location:	Hemlock Lake, Livingston and Ontario Counties
Directions:	From Rochester, head south on Route 15A through the town of Hemlock. In about a mile turn right onto Rix Hill Road for the northern launch area. Or, continue south on 15A for another 7 miles to the southern access road and launch area.
Admission:	Free (permit required)
Route Distance:	About 7 miles each way
Time To Canoe:	About 3 hours (longer if you wish)
Route Conditions:	Calm, open water, but can get rough during windy or stormy weather
Difficulty Level:	1 in calm weather, 2 in stormy weather
Birds Likely Seen:	Variety of ducks, variety of geese, numerous shore birds, herons, eagles, hawks, finches, variety of warblers, wood-peckers, nuthatches, chickadees, titmice and thrushes
Other Uses:	Fishing, hunting, snowshoeing and cross-country skiing (swimming is not allowed)
Contact:	City of Rochester 7412 Rix-Hill Road, Hemlock, NY 14466 (716) 367-3160

Hemlock Lake is a small lake, about 7 miles long, with two launch sites. At the south end, launching a canoe or kayak during low water conditions (particularly late summer or autumn) may be difficult because of the mud. But, also due to this shallow water, shorebirds abound at the south end, and your chance of seeing eagles is good. If you like fishing, try for bass along the shoreline. For trout, troll the deeper water.

The north launch is always deep enough for easy launching. From this area, head south on the lake. The northernmost portion of Hemlock Lake is restricted to authorized personnel only.

Date:
Birds Seen:

Other Observations:

27.

Canadice Lake — Trail

Location:	Canadice Lake, Ontario County
Directions:	From Route 15A, turn east on Purcell Hill Road and head 1 mile to the lake. Parking is shortly past Canadice Hollow Road, on the left. Or, continue on Purcell Hill Road. Turn right (S) on Canadice Lake Road and watch for the parking area at the south end of the lake.
Admission:	Free (permit required)
Trail Distance:	3.7 miles each way
Time To Do Trail:	About 3 hours
Trail Conditions:	A 2-lane dirt and grass path
Trail Markings:	"Hemlock Canadice Watershed" signs
Difficulty Level:	1 parallel to the lake, 3 if you take the side trails, uphill
Birds Likely Seen:	Variety of ducks and geese, shorebirds, herons, hawks, goldfinches, woodpeckers, bluebirds, orioles, variety of warblers, eagles, nuthatches, chickadees, titmice and thrushes
Other Uses:	Restricted boating, fishing, hunting, snowshoeing and cross-country skiing (swimming is not allowed)
Contact:	City of Rochester 7412 Rix-Hill Road, Hemlock, NY 14466 (716) 367-3160

Canadice Lake Trail has abundant wildlife and is a good place for family birdwatching. The main trail parallels the lake on a level, abandoned, gravel road. Other trails loop off the main trail, heading up the hillside into the forest.

Route: With parking at both ends, the Canadice Lake Trail can be walked in either direction. You can start at Purcell Hill Road and go directly south, or start at the south end of the lake. From the southern parking area, head west for about ¼ mile (there's a small, ¼ mile loop trail at the left as well which is a very active birding area in a wooded wetland), then head right (north) and follow the trail adjacent to the lakeshore to Purcell Hill Road.

Watch in the southern marshy area for shorebirds, ducks and perhaps bitterns and herons.

Date:

Birds Seen:

Other Observations:

28.
Canadice Lake — Canoe Route

Location: Canadice Lake, Ontario County

Directions: From Route 15A, turn on Purcell Hill Road and head east about 1 mile to Canadice Lake Road. Turn right and head south about half way down the lake to the boat launch.

Admission: Free (permit required)

Route Distance: About 6 miles around the lake

Time To Canoe: About 3 hours (longer if you wish)

Water Conditions: An open lake

Difficulty Level: 1 (usually a calm lake), 2 (can get choppy in wind)

Birds Likely Seen: Variety of ducks and geese, numerous shorebirds, herons, eagles and hawks

Other Uses: Restricted small craft boating, fishing, hunting, snow-shoeing and cross-country skiing (swimming is not allowed)

Contact: City of Rochester
7412 Rix-Hill Road, Hemlock, NY 14466
(716) 367-3160

Route: Start and return to the boat launch area on the east side of the lake. Because of the accessible launch site and calm, open water, Canadice Lake is a good place for group outings or to introduce children to the joys of birdwatching from a canoe or kayak. See if you can spot the loons that visit this lake.

Explore the marshy area at the south end for shorebirds, ducks and perhaps a glimpse at bitterns and herons. Keep your eye to the sky for possible sightings of eagles and other birds of prey. Watch for deer along the lake shores. (A section of the lake at the northern tip is restricted access only.)

Date:

Birds Seen:

Other Observations:

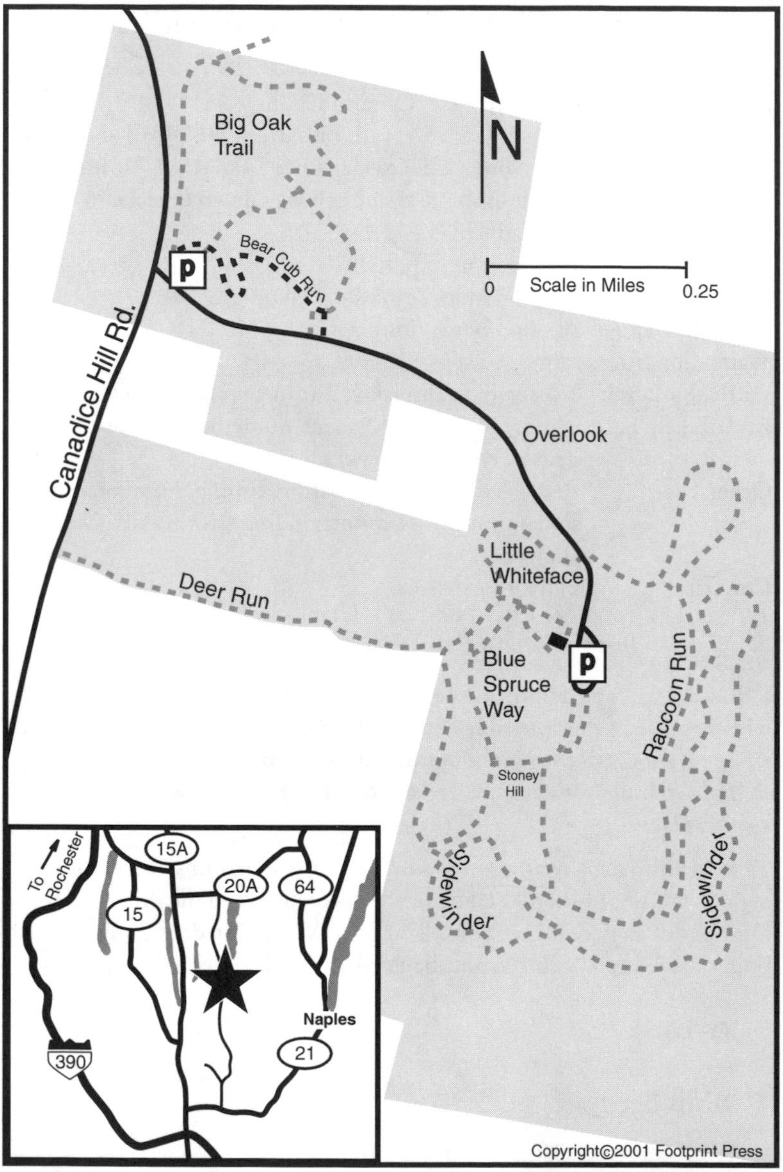

N
0
Scale in Miles
0.25
Big Oak
Trail
Bear Cub Run
Canadice Hill Rd.
Overlook
Little
Whiteface
Deer Run
Blue
Spruce
Way
Raccoon Run
Stoney
Hill
Sidewinder
Sidewinder
To Rochester
15A
20A
64
15
Naples
390
21
Copyright©2001 Footprint Press

Harriet Hollister Spencer Memorial State Recreation Area

29.

Harriet Hollister Spencer Memorial State Recreation Area — Bear Cub Run Trail

Location:	Dansville, Livingston County
Directions:	From Route 390, head east on Route 20A through Livonia. Continue east past Route 15A. Turn south on Canadice Hill Road. Pass Ross Road. Canadice Hill Road will turn to gravel. Turn left at the sign "Harriet Hollister Spencer Memorial Recreation Area." The parking area is on the left near the park entrance.
Admission:	Free
Trail Distance:	About 0.5 mile
Time To Hike:	Approximately 20-30 minutes
Trail Conditions:	Dirt path
Trail Markings:	NY State Forest markers
Difficulty Level:	1
Birds Likely Seen:	Variety of hawks, finches, orioles, woodpeckers, variety of warblers, nuthatches, chickadees, titmice, tanagers and thrushes
Other Uses:	Picnicking, bicycling, cross-country skiing and deer hunting (no small game permitted)
Contact:	Harriet Hollister Spencer Memorial State Recreation Area NYS Office of Parks, Recreation and Historic Preservation Stony Brook State Park 10820 Route 36 South, Dansville, NY 14437 (716) 335-8111

In this area you can see birds while hiking, cross-country skiing, bicycling or driving. There are 8 trails that loop through the park. They range from easy to strenuous.

Route: The Bear Cub Run Trail is a short, easy one. During the summer many birds can be seen and a variety of warblers frequent the area in the spring. Start the trail at the entrance parking lot. The trail heads east and then south. Then it bends to the north and then east again. While walking you might be lucky to see turkey and deer. When the trail merges with the Big Oak Trail, head to the right and shortly the entrance road will appear. Turn around and retrace your steps or turn right and follow the road back to the parking lot. This trail will give you a sense of the area and may inspire you to hike the other trails in this wild park.

While you're here, drive up the park road to the overlook with its fantastic view of Honeoye Lake in the valley far below. Pass the parking lot, and drive into the park until you see the opening on your left. Have your camera ready. Continuing on will take you to the pavilion and the end of the road. Park along the ending loop if you want to explore additional trails.

Date:

Birds Seen:

Other Observations:

A Canada goose wades through the marsh.

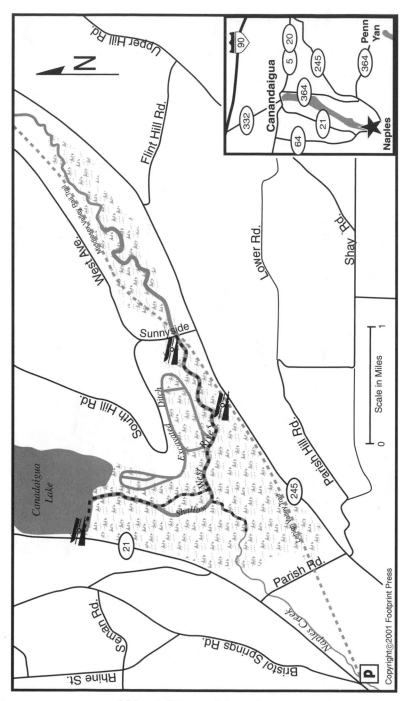

West River Marsh

30.
West River Marsh — Canoe Route

Location: South end of Canandaigua Lake, Naples, Ontario County

Directions: One of the entrances to this area is off Route 21 on the southwest end of Canandaigua Lake at the State Fishing Access Site. You'll find a launch with ample parking. If the lake is rough, you can put in at the West River Fishing Access Site on Route 245 or the West River Fishing Access Site off Sunnyside Road.

Admission: Free

Route Distance: 2.2 miles from Route 21 boat launch to Route 245 boat launch

0.75 mile from Route 245 boat launch to Sunnyside boat launch

5 miles of excavated ditches

Time To Canoe: A few hours to all day

Water Conditions: A combination of open water and a waterway through cattails

Difficulty Level: 1, 2 (weather dependent, the lake can get rough at times)

Birds Likely Seen: Variety of shore birds, bitterns, herons, woodpeckers, blackbirds, finches, warblers, bluebirds, geese, widgeons, mallards, wood ducks, blue-wing and green-wing teal, hooded mergansers, scaups, golden-eyes and, sometimes, gadwal, pintail, shovelers and canvasbacks

Other Uses: Fishing, trapping, boating and hunting

Contact: NYS DEC, Region 8
6274 East Avon-Lima Road, Avon, NY 14414
(716) 226-2466

West River Marsh is a part of the Hi Tor Wildlife Management Area. Hi Tor area covers about 6,100 acres, including high wooded hills, ravines and marshland.

The largest part, near the village of Naples, is mainly steep and wooded with many hiking trails, including a section of the Bristol Hills Branch of the Finger Lakes Trail. Some of these trails are good for birding. A few remote trails have man-made ponds that are stocked with trout.

The smaller area bordering Canandaigua Lake is mostly marsh, and drains Naples Creek and West River. Five miles of ditches have been dug through the marsh to enhance wildlife habitat in the area. The marsh and surrounding potholes are good habitats for waterfowl. The south end of

Canandaigua Lake, next to the wildlife management area, is a major wintering and staging area for waterfowl.

The West River is teeming with bass, while Naples Creek is known for its trout, especially in the spring.

The various habitats within Hi Tor offer excellent birdwatching opportunities and the chance to observe a variety of wildlife such as deer, turkey, grouse, waterfowl, mink and beaver. Otters were recently reintroduced. Public hunting signs identify NYS land. Rules and regulations are posted in most of the parking areas.

According to Indian legend, this area is said to be the birthplace of the Senecas. The Seneca tribe belonged to the Iroquois Confederacy and were known as the "keepers of the western door." The Seneca warriors where highly respected and helped make the Confederacy a strong group.

The trail shown on the map is the Lehigh Valley Trail (also known as the Middlesex Valley Rail Trail). It's an abandoned rail bed which runs through the valley for 6.8 miles from Route 21, northeast to Cayward Cross Road. You can access the trail from the Route 245 and Sunnyside Road boat launch areas. Consider combining your water outing with a hike, or cross-country ski in winter, to find a wider variety of bird species.

Route: After launching (using the Route 21 site), head toward the marsh on your right and paddle about 0.2 mile. Bear left on the man-made channel. (West River is filling with sediment and can be difficult to paddle in low water.) Have your binoculars or camera focused on the cattails as you slowly paddle along. In this habitat, you're likely to see many shore birds, herons, ducks and turkey vultures.

Continue about a mile until you see the channel split. The left channel is West River and the channel on the right is Naples Creek. Both channels are navigable. (If you began at the West River Site, you would arrive at this juncture after paddling 1.25 miles.) The Naples Creek channel offers better bird viewing, especially further upstream in the woods because of the riparian habitat. But, bluebirds have been spotted along the West River. So, if you have time, explore both channels and the excavated ditch loops to the north.

Date:

Birds Seen:

Other Observations:

Routes near Syracuse

Montezuma National Wildlife Refuge (NWR)

Montezuma NWR covers about 8,000 acres, and is one of over 500 National Wildlife Refuges that are administered by the US Fish and Wildlife Service, Department of the Interior. Another refuge in New York is the Iroquois National Wildlife Refuge (see page 57). The purpose of the refuge system is to manage wildlife and wildlife habitat.

In 1937 the Bureau of Biological Survey (now known as the US Fish and Wildlife Service) purchased 6,432 acres of former marshland and named it Montezuma National Wildlife Refuge. Since then the refuge has grown to its present size. The refuge and NYS DEC's Northern Montezuma Wildlife Management Area and private property comprise the larger Montezuma Wetlands Complex (MWC). As NY's flagship project under the North American Waterfowl Management Plan, the MWC seeks to restore, enhance and manage for wildlife 36,000 acres of the historic Montezuma marshes (50,000 acres). Other partners involved in the MWC include Ducks Unlimited, The Nature Conservancy, National Audubon Society, local conservationist organizations and private land owners.

Visitors take advantage of this area throughout the year. Many hope to see eagles and osprey in the marsh. In spring and fall they come to see the migration of birds. Montezuma is a major stop for migrating birds in the Atlantic Flyway. The refuge contains two observation towers that make birdwatching and photography fun and easy.

Spring migration of waterfowl occurs from late February through April when 85,000 Canada geese, 12,000 snow geese, and many species of ducks use Montezuma as their northbound resting spot. Best viewing times are early morning and late afternoon. Warblers migrate through the area around the second week in May and can best be viewed from Esker Brook Nature Trail from dawn until mid-morning. April through June is wildflower season. Watch for violets, trilliums, mayapples, vetches, and mustards along the trail.

Summer is the time for waterfowl nesting. Broods of Canada geese and ducks begin to appear in early March. Late July is peak season for the blooms of purple loosestrife (a non-native, invasive plant), wild iris (blue flag), mallow, and water lily.

Fall begins the southern migration. From mid-September until freeze-up, 50,000 Canada geese and 150,000 ducks pass through the area. For shorebirds and wading birds, peak migration is mid-September. Again, they're best viewed in early morning or late afternoon.

The most heavily used section is the seasonal 3.5-mile automobile Wildlife Drive around the main pool. This is great for small children, elders or handicapped people who can watch wildlife without getting out of their vehicle.

Boating and fishing are prohibited in the refuge, but the refuge maintains a boat launch providing access to Cayuga-Seneca Canal where you can canoe and fish. Call ahead for information or check at the visitor center for rules, regulations and permits. This also applies to waterfowl and deer hunting on the refuge. (Hearing impaired visitors may call the Massachusetts Relay Center at 1-800-439-2370.)

So why is a marsh in upstate New York called Montezuma? In the early 1800s Dr. Peter Clark, a physician from New York City, came to the area because of the salt deposits recently discovered under the marshes. He built a 12-room home (a mansion for the times) on a drumlin with a view of the marshes. Dr. Clark had traveled extensively and named his estate Montezuma in honor of the last Aztec emperor and the large marshes that surrounded Mexico City.

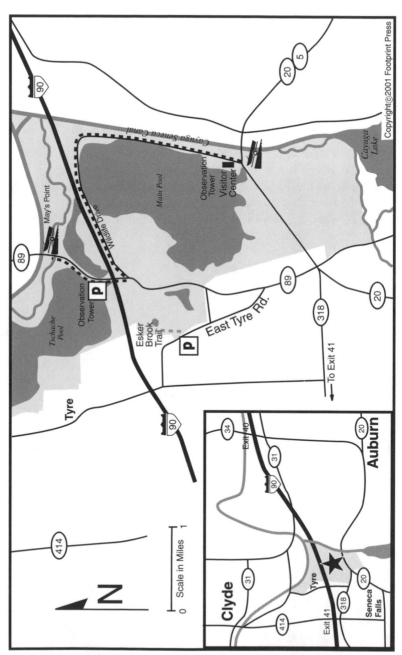

Montezuma National Wildlife Refuge

31.
Montezuma NWR — Wildlife Drive

Location:	Seneca Falls, Seneca County
Directions:	Take I-90 to exit 41 and head east on Route 318. Turn left on Routes 5 & 20 and look for the entrance sign to Montezuma NWR on the left. Wildlife Drive begins at the visitor center.
Admission:	Free
Route Distance:	3.5 miles on the self-guided drive
Time To Drive:	Approximately 30 minutes
Route Conditions:	Dirt and gravel road
Route Markings:	Interpretive signs along the roadway teach about birds and their habitat
Difficulty Level:	1
Birds Likely Seen:	Variety of ducks, variety of geese, numerous shore birds, swans, herons, grebes, occasionally pelicans, eagles, hawks, finches, bluebirds, orioles, variety of warblers, woodpeckers, nuthatches, chickadees, titmice, and thrushes
Other Uses:	Cross-country skiing and hunting (permit required)
Contact:	Montezuma National Wildlife Refuge 3395 Route 5 & 20 East, Seneca Falls, NY 13148 (315)-568-5987 www.fws.gov/r5mnwr

Montezuma Wildlife Drive is a one-way drive around the main pool. It starts at the visitor center area. Check the displays at the visitor center and climb the observation tower before your drive.

Then head north and keep your binoculars or camera ready. Many waterfowl and herons are in this section. For half its distance the drive heads west, parallel to the NYS Thruway. Along this section you should continue to see waterfowl and herons, plus many birds of prey. Wildlife Drive ends at Route 89.

At this point you can turn left and head south to leave and return to Routes 5 & 20. Or, turn right, cross I-90 to the Tschache Pool observation tower and May's Point fishing area.

Date:

Birds Seen:

Other Observations:

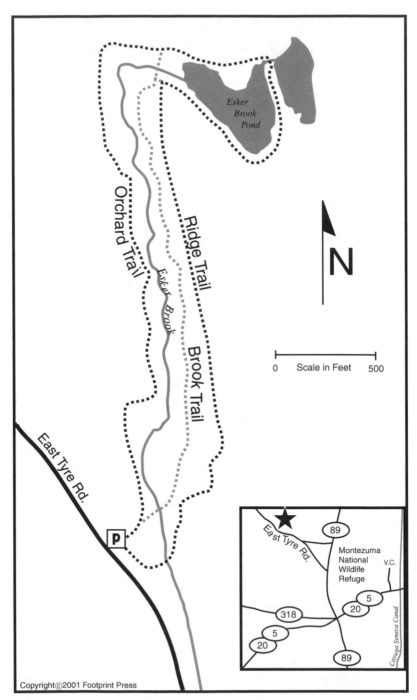

Esker Brook Trail

32.
Montezuma NWR — Esker Brook Trail

Location:	Seneca Falls, Seneca County
Directions:	Take I-90 to exit 41 and head east on Route 318. Turn left on Routes 5 & 20, and left (N) on Route 89. After 0.25 mile turn left (W) on East Tyre Road. A gravel parking area for Esker Brook Trail will be on the right.
Admission:	Free
Trail Distance:	1.5-mile loop
Time To Hike:	Approximately 30 minutes
Trail Conditions:	Grass and dirt trail
Trail Markings:	Signs at intersections
Difficulty Level:	2
Birds Likely Seen:	Hawks, finches, bluebirds, orioles, woodpeckers, variety of warblers, nuthatches, chickadees, titmice, and thrushes
Other Uses:	Cross-country skiing and hunting (permit required)
Contact:	Montezuma National Wildlife Refuge 3395 Route 5 & 20 East, Seneca Falls, NY 13148 (315)-568-5987 www.fws.gov/r5mnwr

If you are looking for great sightings of warblers, the second week of May is the perfect time to hike this easy trail. Three parallel routes follow Esker Brook then end by circling Esker Brook Pond. Esker Brook Trail is closed between October and January.

Date:

Birds Seen:

Other Observations:

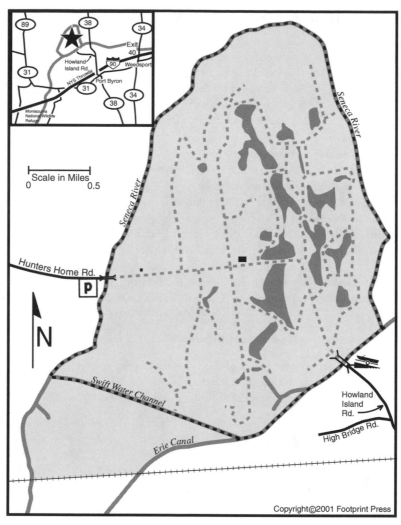

Howland Island Wildlife Management Area

33.
Howland Island Wildlife Management Area
— Canoe Loop

Location:	Port Byron, Cayuga County
Directions:	Take I-90 to exit 40 (Weedsport). Turn right on Route 34 south, then Route 31 west. In Port Byron, turn right on Route 38 and head north 2 miles. Turn left (W) on Howland Island Road. Park at the end of Howland Island Road (along the road) near the bridge over the Erie Canal which is now open only to pedestrians.
Admission:	Free
Route Distance:	About 8.5 miles
Time To Canoe:	Approximately 2.5 hours
Route Conditions:	Slow moving waterways
Difficulty Level:	1
Birds Likely Seen:	Variety of ducks, geese, shorebirds, swans, herons, hawks, finches, variety of warblers, woodpeckers and thrushes
Other Uses:	Hiking, hunting and trapping
Contact:	NYS DEC, Region 7
	1285 Fisher Avenue, Cortland, NY 13045
	(607)-753-3095, ext. 247

Howland Island Wildlife Management Area is a 3,600 acre island, with the Seneca River and Erie Canal as its boundaries. The purpose of the area is to manage wildlife, wildlife habitat and primarily waterfowl reproduction. Monies derived from hunting license fees and federal taxes on ammunition help achieve this goal.

In 1932 Howland Island was purchased as a game refuge. Between 1933 and 1941 a Civilian Conservation Corps camp was established, and 18 earthen dikes were built to create 300 acres of water impoundments. Howland Island is also part of the larger Montezuma Wetlands Complex.

All hunting and trapping at Howland Island is in accordance with the respective statewide regulations. Canoeing and fishing are allowed on the boundary waters.

Visitors take advantage of this area, especially in the summer, with the hope of seeing its 220 species of birds, 108 of which breed locally. This is an especially nice place for photographing wildlife and wildlife habitat. Go take advantage of its uniqueness.

This circular route offers a variety of birds. Much of the route is open so be sure to use sunscreen. Don't forget your binoculars, camera or fishing gear (try fishing around any pilings and shallows).

Route: Carry your boat downhill to the water from the right side of the road (facing the bridge). Once on the water, head left (SW). Go about 1 mile, then head right, and enter Swift Water Channel (a misnomer since the water does not run swiftly). Go about 1.5 miles, then turn right into the Seneca River. Go another 2 miles, and you'll start heading east. Continue another 1.5 miles, and you'll start looping to the south. Watch for a variety of birds, including birds of prey. In another 2.5 miles you'll come back to the canal. Turn right. The bridge is just ahead.

If you have time, walk the trails around the manmade waterholes on the island. Many waterfowl take advantage of these waterholes during migration.

Date:

Birds Seen:

Other Observations:

Beaver Lake Nature Center

Beaver Lake is a 650-acre park with a 9-mile network of trails and a 200-acre lake dedicated to discovering the outdoors. Canoe rental is available on a first-come, first-served basis at the visitor center, usually around mid-May to Labor Day. Be sure to call ahead about canoe times, regulations and when canoes are allowed on the water.

The park has maple sugaring in March and snowshoeing or cross-country skiing in the winter. The park also features moonlight treks until 10 PM during the winter. You can follow that with a hot chocolate at the visitor center. Snowshoes can be rented at the center on a first-come, first-served basis. They cannot be reserved.

The park hosts over 400 workshops and events yearly. They include the spring Wildlife Art Weekend and the fall Golden Harvest Festival. The trails are open every day except Christmas, from 7:30 AM to dusk. (The visitor center opens at 8:00 AM). Bikes and motorized vehicles are not allowed on the trails. Pets, fires, collecting, fishing and swimming are prohibited at Beaver Lake.

James Miles and Michael Peter
enjoy a day of birdwatching.

The visitor center has taxidermy displays and a gift shop. This park was designed for family fun, and is truly a year-round outdoor hot spot. Its birdwatching opportunities are exceptional on land and water.

The visitor center is handicapped accessible, and the Lakeview Trail is built to accommodate wheelchairs.

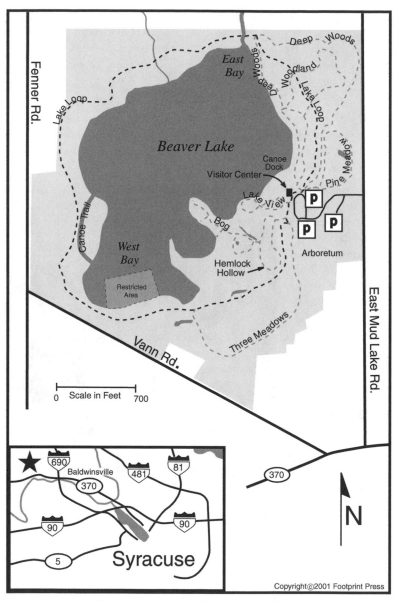

Beaver Lake Nature Center

34.

Beaver Lake Nature Center — Lake Loop Trail

Location: Baldwinsville, Onondaga County

Directions: From I-90 (exit 39) take Route 690 north to the second Baldwinsville exit. Head west on Route 370 for 2 miles and turn right (N) on Mud Lake Road. The nature center entrance will be on the left.

Admission: $1.00 per vehicle

Trail Distance: 3 mile loop

Time To Hike: Approximately 2 hours

Trail Conditions: Bark mulch trail and boardwalks

Trail Markings: Black and white signs on posts

Difficulty Level: 1

Birds Likely Seen: Variety of ducks, geese, herons, birds of prey, woodpeckers, nuthatches, chickadees, titmice, bluebirds, tanagers, finches, wrens, variety of warblers and thrushes

Other Park Uses: Canoe rental, cross-country skiing and snowshoeing

Contact: Onondaga County Parks
Beaver Lake Nature Center
8477 East Mud Lake Road, Baldwinsville, NY 13027
(315) 638-2519

The Lake Loop Trail will take you through a variety of habitats that provide numerous opportunities for bird observations.

Route: Start the trail at the visitor center and follow signs for the Lake Loop Trail. You can go in either direction around Beaver Lake.

If you want to explore further, combine Lake Loop Trail with the other seven trails. A good one to consider is the Bog Trail, which has an elevated boardwalk. You should spot many warblers, and you can use the telescope on the observation tower to take advantage of breathtaking views on and around the lake. Another good choice is the Lakeview Trail. This is wheelchair accessible, and also has telescopes at the water's edge. And don't forget those special moonlight treks during the winter.

Date:

Birds Seen:

Other Observations:

35.

Beaver Lake Nature Center — Canoe Route

Location: Baldwinsville, Onondaga County

Directions: From I-90 (exit 39) take Route 690 north to the second Baldwinsville exit. Head west on Route 370 for 2 miles and turn right (N) on Mud Lake Road. The nature center entrance will be on the left.

Admission: $1.00 per vehicle

Route Distance: 2 miles

Time To Do Route: 2 hours

Route Conditions: Shoreline of a mile-long glacial lake plus a 0.25-mile canoe trail past a beaver lodge and through a wetland. It can be windy on the open lake.

Route Markings: None

Difficulty Level: 1

Birds Likely Seen: Variety of gulls, caspian terns, herons, birds of prey, woodpeckers, kingbirds, yellow warblers, cedar waxwings

Other Park Uses: Hiking, cross-country skiing and snowshoeing

Contact: Onondaga County Parks
Beaver Lake Nature Center
8477 East Mud Lake Road, Baldwinsville, NY 13027
(315) 638-2519

Bring your own canoe or kayak to ply the waters of Beaver Lake or rent a canoe ($8/hour) at the visitor center. Rental is on a first-come, first-served basis. Call ahead (315-638-2519) to make sure boating is allowed when you plan to come and check in at the nature center before launching. The Beaver Lake canoeing season begins the second weekend of May for weekend paddling. Weekday paddling begins the last week of June. All paddling ends on Labor Day.

Route: From the curb in front of the visitor center, it's a 200-yard carry to the canoe dock in east bay of the lake. You can paddle in any direction. If you paddle the lakeshore counterclockwise, look for the "Canoe Trail" entrance sign in the west bay. After exiting the canoe trail, cross the south end of the lake to explore the two southeast bays before completing the full circle back to the canoe dock.

Date:

Birds Seen:

Other Observations:

124

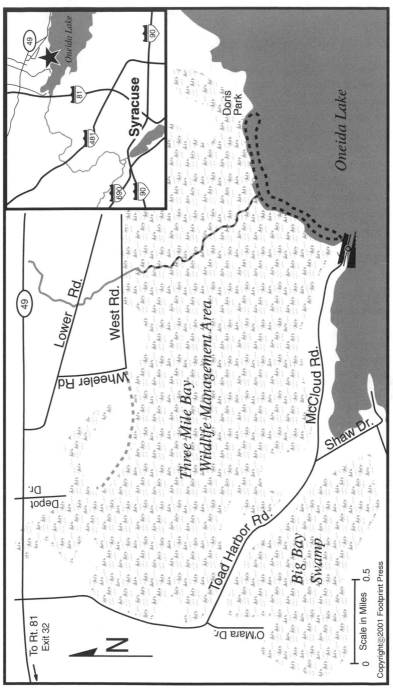

Three Mile Bay Wildlife Management Area

36.

Three Mile Bay Wildlife Management Area
— Canoe Route

Location: West Monroe, Oswego County
Directions: Take I-81 to exit 32. Then, take Route 49 east about
                     2.5 miles and look for Greenview Country Club. Turn
                     right on Toad Harbor Road and head south. Turn
                     left at McCloud Road. Part of McCloud Road is a dirt
                     road and ends at Phillips Point. Park at the fishing
                     access site.
Admission: Free
Route Distance: About 1.25 miles each way
Time To Canoe: Approximately 2.5 hours
Route Conditions: Open water, Oneida Lake and Three Mile Bay can
                     get rough with white caps
Difficulty Level: 1, 2 (be aware of occasional stormy conditions or
                     rough water)
Birds Likely Seen: Variety of ducks, geese, shorebirds, terns, gulls,
                     herons, bitterns, birds of prey, coots, grebes, blackbirds
                     and woodpeckers
Other Uses: Hiking (from Wheeler Road), hunting and trapping
Contact: NYS DEC, Region 7
                     1285 Fisher Avenue, Cortland, NY 13045
                     (607) 753-3095, ext. 247

Three Mile Bay WMA consists of 3,500 acres adjacent to Three Mile Bay, off Oneida Lake's northwest shore. Initial acreage was acquired in the 1950s from the Pittman Robertson Funds (monies derived from hunting license fees and federal taxes on ammunition). Additional acreage was purchased using the Recreational Bond Act.

The purpose of the area is to provide habitat for a variety of wildlife, with primary emphasis on waterfowl species. The majority of this area is hardwood swamp. Much of it is low and flat and contains several ridges or islands that spread across the interior. Higher spots are only 25 to 30 feet above Oneida Lake.

Many species of birds can be found in this area, especially in the summer. The open water of Three Mile Bay causes many birders to go to Phillips Point. But, with a canoe, a better combination of birds can be found on the bay and in the area's other wildlife habitats. It's a good place to find terns, and opportunities abound for close-up photography.

Canoeing and fishing are allowed on the boundary water. You can launch at the Phillips Point access site. At present, big and small game hunting and trapping at Three Mile Bay is in accordance with the respective statewide regulations, and permits are not required.

This is a good route for open water and marsh birds. The open water can get rough so use good judgement in questionable weather and be sure to use sunscreen.

Route: Put in and start paddling to the northeast. Along this section you should see a variety of birds. At about 0.5 miles a waterway will appear on your left. Head into this area and explore. At about 1.25 miles you'll come to the boundary end at Doris Park. Retrace your route back to the beginning.

If you have time, explore the management area off Wheeler Road by walking the trail.

Date:

Birds Seen:

Other Observations:

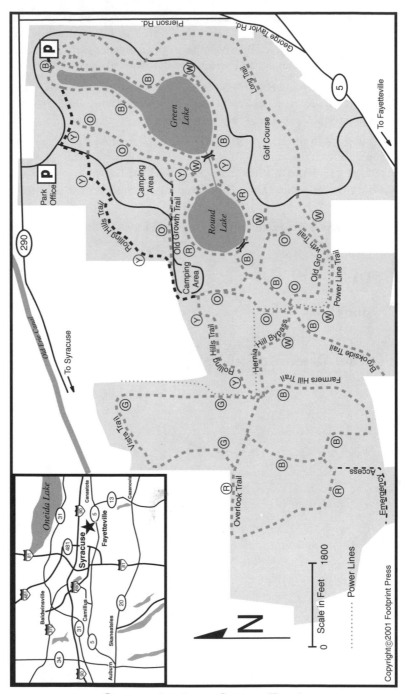

Green Lakes State Park

37.

Green Lakes State Park — Rolling Hills Trail

Location: Fayetteville, Onondaga County

Directions: Take I-90 to exit 34A then go south on I-481 to exit 5-E (Kirkville Road East). Turn right on Fremont Road, then left on Route 290 and follow signs to the park. Turn right into the park, pass the park office and park at the beach parking lot.

Admission: $6/vehicle between 9 AM and 5 PM from Memorial Day through Labor Day

Trail Distance: 1.8 miles (can be hiked, bicycled, or cross-country skied)

Time To Hike: Approximately 90 minutes

Trail Conditions: Trail is moderately hilly, through fields and woods

Trail Markings: Yellow blazes

Difficulty Level: 2

Birds Likely Seen: American goldfinches, robins and other thrushes, various types of warblers, woodpeckers, sparrows, whitebreasted nuthatches, chickadees, titmice, indigo buntings, scarlet tanagers, northern orioles (Pick up a bird checklist at the park office.)

Other Park Uses: Cabins, camping, hiking, biking, picnicking, golf, swimming, boat rental, snowshoeing and cross-country skiing

Contact: Green Lakes State Park
7900 Green Lakes Road, Fayetteville, NY 13066
(315) 637-6111

The park was established in 1928. It has two glacially formed lakes, and rolling, wooded hills. Green Lake and Round Lake are two of a few lakes in the US that are meromictic. There is no spring or fall turnover as occurs in most lakes, so the surface water of meromictic lakes does not mix with the bottom water. Another meromictic lake is Devil's Bathtub in Mendon Ponds Park (see page 82). Also unique, is the color of the water, hence the name of the park. Because the lakes are very clear, the green and blue wavelengths from visible light are able to penetrate to a great depth and are scattered and transmitted back to the observer's eye.

This park contains a golf course and has campsites and cabins. Many of the trails allow multiple uses. The beach and bathhouse are well kept. Only rental rowboats and paddleboats (no private boats) are allowed on the water. You can rent them at the beach.

Route: Start your excursion by checking out the color of the water and exploring the beach area. The start of the trail is at the west side of the beach parking area. Head west to the campground area road and turn left on the Rolling Hills Trail. Head southwest and look for goldfinches. About half way to Rolling Hills Campground make a quick right and loop to the left around the campground area. At the far side of the camp area you have a choice to continue the Rolling Hills Trail to the right or head south on the more difficult Old Growth Trail, then the Power Line Trail, as they loop back to the Old Growth Trail and camping area.

If you stay with the Rolling Hills Trail, go about 0.75 miles and you'll have another choice to make. Take the trail back the way you came or turn right and pick up the combinations of the Vista Trail, Overlook Trail and Farmers Hill Trail (where you may find bluebirds), which are easy to moderate in difficulty.

Additional trails in Green Lakes State Park:

Name	Distance	Difficulty	Use
Green Lake Trail	2.3 miles	1	Hiking only
Round Lake Trail	0.8 miles	1	Hiking only
Power Line Trail	1.0 mile	3	Hike/bike
Brookside Trail	0.3 miles	1	Hiking only
Rolling Hills Trail	1.8 miles	2	Hike/bike
Farmer's Hill Trail	1.4 miles	1	Hike/bike
Overlook Trail	1.1 miles	1	Hike/bike
Vista Trail	1.4 miles	3	Hike/bike

Date:

Birds Seen:

Other Observations:

Routes near Ithaca

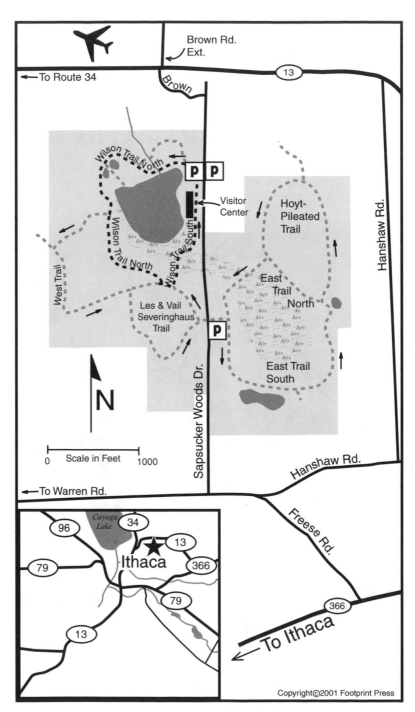

Sapsucker Woods

38.
Cornell Lab of Ornithology,
Sapsucker Woods — Wilson Trail

Location:	Sapsucker Woods Road, Ithaca, Tompkins County
Directions:	Take Route 13 North, heading east out of Ithaca. Turn right on Warren Road. Then turn left on Hanshaw Road and left on Sapsucker Woods Drive. Sapsucker Woods parking area will be on the left.
Admission:	Free
Trail Distance:	0.75 miles
Time To Hike:	Approximately 30 minutes
Trail Conditions:	Mulched trails
Trail Markings:	None
Difficulty Level:	1
Birds Likely Seen:	Ducks, geese, finches, robins, warblers, woodpeckers, nuthatches, chickadees, titmice, vireos and thrushes
Other Uses:	None
Contact:	Cornell Lab of Ornithology
	159 Sapsucker Woods Road, Ithaca, NY 14850-1999
	(607) 254-2440
	http://birds.cornell.edu

If you know anything about birds, you've most likely heard about the Cornell Lab of Ornithology. Its reputation is world-renowned. We're fortunate to have it in our region of New York State. Its research facilities and on-going programs involving the public have a dramatic impact on helping birds.

A few of these programs are:
- Project Feeder Watch—People monitor their backyard feeders and provide information on bird visits to the lab.
- The House Finch Disease Survey—People monitor the house finch and other birds for an eye disease and give relevant data to the lab. This is often done in conjunction with Project Feeder Watch.
- The Birdhouse Network—This is a monitoring program for bird nest boxes, such as those on bluebird trails.

Contact the lab if any of these programs interest you. Inside the Sapsucker Woods Sanctuary is the Stuart Observatory, which features a large viewing window overlooking birdfeeders and a pond. A microphone picks up the bird sounds at the feeders so you can sit in warmth and comfort, watching and listening to the birds. The observatory also contains an extensive bird library and one of the best collections of original artwork by Louis Agassiz Fuertes in the world.

Outside, the trails at Sapsucker Woods are easy to walk and offer excellent birdwatching opportunities. It's a great area for families. Because this habitat is designed to nurture birds, picnics and pets are not allowed.

Route: Start the Wilson Trail at the north end of the parking lot. Open the gate and be sure to close it behind you. Bear left and loop around the pond and marsh area. Watch the ducks in the pond and look for deer. Half way along the trail, you have the option of staying on the Wilson Trail or extending your walk by covering the West Trail and the Les and Vail Severinghaus Trail. When you finish your walk, don't forget to close the gate behind you. On the other side of the road are the East Trail and the Hoyt-Pileated Trail, two additional fine hiking trails.

Additional trails in Sapsucker Woods:

Name	Distance	Difficulty	Use
West Trail	0.5 mile	1	Hiking only
Severinghaus Trail	0.3 mile	1	Hiking only
East Trail	0.7 mile	1	Hiking only
Hoyt-Pileated Trail	0.3 mile	1	Hiking only

Date:

Birds Seen:

Other Observations:

Routes near Binghamton

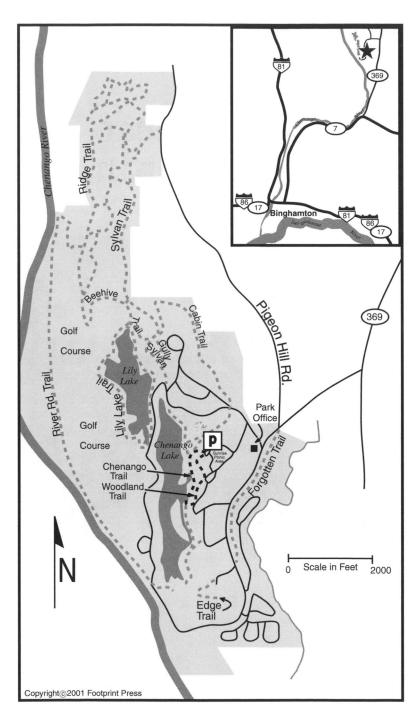

Chenango Valley State Park

39.

Chenango Valley State Park — Woodland Trail

Location: Chenango Forks, Broome County

Directions: Take I-81 to I-88 east and exit at Port Crane (exit 3). Turn left on Route 369. After 4 miles turn left at the park entrance sign. Proceed through the gate and park at the Sunrise Picnic Area.

Admission: $6/vehicle charge between 9 AM and 5 PM from Memorial Day through Labor Day

Route Distance: Approximately 0.75 mile

Time To Hike: 1 Hour

Trail Conditions: A moderately difficult trail, a steep section with rocks and roots is between stations 6 and 7

Trail Marking: Park markers

Difficulty Level: 2, 3

Birds Likely Seen: Woodpeckers, warblers, wood thrushes, nuthatches, chickadees, wrens and titmice

Other Uses: Camping, cabins, swimming, biking, canoeing, golfing, fishing, hiking trails (more than a dozen)

Contact: NYS Parks and Recreation
Chenango Valley State Park
153 State Park Road, Chenango Forks, NY 13746
(607) 648-5251

The Chenango River flows into the Susquehanna River at Binghamton. The rivers and their valleys are rich in history and Indian lore. On Hiawatha Island in the Susquehanna River, near Owego, a young chief, Hiawatha, had a vision. He was told to bring the leaders of the tribes together to a high spot on the island. When they were assembled, he drew an arrow from his quiver and showed them how easily it broke in two. Then he drew five more arrows from his quiver. He bound them together and showed them how difficult they were to break. Then he said; "Singly, you are men of willow. Together, you are men of oak." Thus, legend says, began the Iroquois Confederacy, a uniting of five Indian tribes. Historians call this early government "the greatest achievement of Stone Age man" because of its extensive code of laws.

Today the area is abundantly full of birds and other wildlife. Chenango Valley State Park has many trails to explore. The Edge Trail is handicapped accessible. Pick up a self-guided nature tour pamphlet at the park office to learn about this area where field and forest meet. The Woodland Trail has easy access and is moderately difficult. It is mainly through woods and has a little of everything the park affords. The route described returns via the Chenango Lake Trail.

Canoeing (no motors) is allowed on Chenango Lake from April 15 through September 15. But a weekly ($5) or yearly ($15) permit is required. You could spend many days in this park to enjoy all of the attractions.

Route: Enter the Woodland Trail near the small road loop on your right as you face the Sunrise Picnic Area. Start at the left side of the road loop. The right side is the return portion of the trail. Proceed as the trail turns southerly to the left for about 0.4 mile. Continue to where the trail links with the Chenango Lake Trail. Keep your eyes and ears open for birds. Turn right and head north along the lake for about 0.4 mile. Then turn right, on the Woodland Trail. Continue to stay to the right for about 0.1 mile to return to the starting point.

Additional trails in Chenango Valley State Park:

Name	Distance	Difficulty	Use
Chenango Lake Trail	2.3 miles	3	Hiking only
Cabin Trail	1.2 miles	1	Hike/bike
Edge Trail	0.6 mile	1	Wheelchair accessible
Forgotten Trail	0.6 mile	1	Hike/bike
Gully Trail	0.2 mile	3	Hike/bike
Lilly Lake Trail	1.5 miles	3	Hiking only
Ridge Trail	0.9 mile	2	Hike/bike
River Road Trail	3.0 miles	2	Hike/bike
Sylvan Trail	2.5 miles	3	Hike/bike

Date:

Birds Seen:

Other Observations:

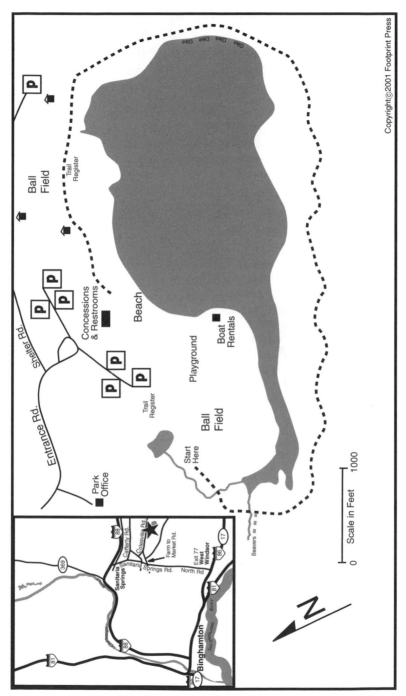

Nathaniel Cole Park

40.

Nathaniel Cole Park — Lakeview Trail

Location: Colesville Road, Colesville, Broome County

Directions: Take exit 77 from Route 17 at West Windsor. Head north on North Road for about 3 miles. Turn right on Farm to Market Road then right on Colesville Road. The park entrance will be on your right in 2 miles. Head to the far end of the west parking lot.

Admission: Free

Trail Distance: 1.25 miles

Time On Trail: 45 to 60 minutes

Trail Conditions: Easy walking

Difficulty Level: 1

Birds Likely Seen: Nuthatches, titmice, woodpeckers, brown creepers, chickadees, wood thrushes, bluebirds, warblers, hawks and a variety of ducks

Other Uses: Swimming and boat rental

Contact: Nathaniel Cole Park
1674 Colesville Road, Harpursville, NY 13787
(607) 693-1389

Broome County Parks and Recreation
PO Box 1766, Binghamton, NY 13902
(607) 778-2193   www.tier.net/bcparks

Nathaniel Cole was a Revolutionary War veteran who settled with his family in 1795. He ran a tavern which was a stoping point for stagecoaches on their way from from Binghamton to Albany. Part of Mr. Coles' property is now Nathaniel Cole Park. Today, Lakeview Trail offers a shady retreat from the summer sun as it circles a small lake. Visit the boat rental area if you'd like to look for birds from the lake.

Route: Sign the register as you walk west toward the trail. After the trail enters the woods, it will loop toward the outlet. When you near the bridge you can go to the right and hopefully see beaver in the marshy area, or continue on the trail as it winds around the lake. Watch for woodpeckers and the other woodland birds. When the trail comes out of the woods, near the dike, you may see bluebirds in the fields. Also watch for buteo hawks trying to find a meal. Continue around the lake, and end your walk at the concession area.

Date:
Birds Seen:
Other Observations:

Birding Organizations and Birdwatching Clubs

The following bird related organizations could use your participation. Consider joining them to enjoy birdwatching with others and to help ensure the proliferation of bird populations.

Far West Area

Roger Tory Peterson Institute
RTP1 Ornithological Club
311 Curtis Street, Jamestown, NY 14701-9620
(716) 655-2473, (800) 758-6841
http://www.rtpi.org

Jamestown Audubon Society
1600 Riverside Road, Jamestown, NY 14701-9340
(716) 569-2345

Allegany County Birdwatching Club
5 John Street
Belmont, NY 14813
(716) 268-9293

Lake Erie Bird Club
(716) 672-7363

Cattaraugus County Bird Study Club
(716) 945-2539

Buffalo Area

Buffalo Audubon Society
712 Main Street, Buffalo, NY 14202
(716) 842-0558

Rochester Area

Braddock Bay Raptor Research
432 Manitou Road, Hilton, NY 14468
(716) 392-5685
http://www.bbrr.com
e-mail bbrr@ix.netcom.com

Burroughs Audubon Nature Club
PO Box 17164, Rochester, NY 14617

Rochester Birding Association
39 Mason Road, Fairport, NY 14450
(716) 546-8030
www.rochesterbirding.com

Genesee Ornithological Society
PO Box 25156, Rochester, NY 14625

Birding Organizations and Birdwatching Clubs

Finger Lakes Area

Eaton Birding Society
PO Box 928, Geneva, NY 14456

Syracuse Area

Onondaga Audubon Society
PO Box 620, Syracuse, NY 13201
(315) 637-0318
http://www.onondagaaudubon.org

Ithaca/Cortland Area

Cornell Lab of Ornithology
159 Sapsucker Woods Road, Ithaca, NY 14850-1999
(607) 254-2440, (607) 254-2473
http://birds.cornell.edu

Cortland County Bird Club
Lime Hollow Nature Center
3091Gracie Road, Cortland, NY 13045-9355
(607) 758-5462

Elmira Area

Chemung Valley Audubon Society
PO Box 663, Elmira, NY 14902

Binghamton Area

Naturalist Club of Broome County
PO Box 191, Vestal, NY 13851-0191
(607) 798-1919
http://www.Natureclub@tier.net

Tioga Bird Club
2027 Day Hollow Road, Owego, NY 13827

New York State

NYS Bluebird Society
1062 Edgemere Drive, Rochester, NY 14612
(716) 865-2913

The Nature Conservancy
Central & Western New York Chapter
339 East Avenue, Suite 300, Rochester, NY 14604-2615
(716) 546-8030
http://www.tnc.org/states/newyork/centralwest

Federation of New York State Bird Clubs
PO Box 440, Loch Sheldrake, NY 12759
http://birds.cornell.edu/fnysbc/index.html

National Audubon Society of New York
(518) 869-9731
http://ny.audubon.org

National

Ducks Unlimited
Department HM
One Waterfowl Way, Memphis, TN 38120
http://www.azdu.org/links.htm

National Wild Turkey Federation
P.O. Box 530, Edgefield, SC 29824-0530
(800) 843-6983
http://www.nwtf.com/

Personal Birding Log

Date	Bird Seen	Where	Other Comments

Personal Birding Log

Date	Bird Seen	Where	Other Comments

Recommended Reading

Audubon Society Field Guide to North American Birds (East), published by Alfred A. Knoph, Inc., wild bird identification guide using photographs of the birds

Birders World, published by Kalmbach Publishing Company, an informational magazine on wild birds

Encyclopedia Britannica, published by Encyclopedia Britannica, basic information about history and life of birds

How To Attract Birds, published by Ortho Books, a guide to attracting and enjoying wild birds

Kaufman Focus Guide to Birds of North America, by Ken Kaufman, published by Houghton Mifflin Company, wild bird identification guide using paintings and photographs of the birds

Living Bird, published by Cornell Lab of Ornithology, an informational magazine on wild birds

National Audubon Society - The Sibley Guide to Birds, by David Allen Sibley, published by Random House, detailed illustration and text on wild birds

Peterson's Field Guide to the Birds (East), by Roger Tory Peterson, published by Houghton Mifflin Company, wild bird identification guide using paintings of the birds

Stokes Identification Field Guide (East), by Don and Lillian Stokes, Published by Little, Brown and Company, wild bird identification guide using photographs of the birds

The Backyard Bird Watcher, by George Harrison, published by Willow Creek Press, a guide to watching wild birds in your backyard

Glossary

Accipiter Hawk — Short-winged, long-tailed hawks that are capable of fast maneuvering and flying easily among trees. They like hunting songbirds and are common around bird feeders.

Banding Blind — A building where people conceal themselves while netting birds for banding.

Birds of Prey — Flesh eating birds such as hawks, owls, falcons, etc.

Buteo Hawk — Long-winged, short-tailed hawks. They are soaring hawks most commonly found in open areas. They like hunting for rabbits and small animals.

Eye Relief — Adjustable rubber cups on top of binoculars which allow better viewing for people wearing eyeglasses.

DEC — Department of Environmental Conservation

Downrigger — A fishing apparatus that allows you to put lures or bait at different depths.

Exit Pupil Diameter — This diameter, given in millimeters, is a rating number for binoculars. Hold the binoculars at arms length, and look at the bottom lens. The circle of light you see, is the EPD. Using 7x35 and 10x23 binoculars for comparison, the diameter number is derived when the first number is divided into the second number; i.e., 7x35=(5) 10 into 23=(2.3). A diameter of 5mm gathers more viewable light area than the 2.3mm.

Field of View — The number of viewable feet at 1000 yards; such as, (350ft/1000 yards) or (500ft/1000 yards).

Habitat — Areas containing all the essential things for life: water, food, shelter and a place to raise young. The habitat requirements for birds vary. Some birds prefer woods, others wetlands, etc.

IBA — Important Bird Area. See page 18.

Molting — When a bird looses its feathers.

Meromictic Lake — Deep glacially formed lakes without water inflow and outflow channels. The thermal waters of surface and bottom layers do not turnover, as in normal lakes.

Morph — Some birds have different coloration within their species. This is another way of saying color phase.

NWR — National Wildlife Refuge

OPRHP — Office of Parks, Recreation and Historic Preservation

Owl Pellets — Owls regurgitate indigestible leftovers after feeding. These compressed balls usually contain bones and hair.

Passerine Birds — This is a name given to perching birds.

Potholes — Small, open water pockets within a marsh.

Rafts of Ducks — Many ducks (such as scaup, golden-eye, etc.) floating in open water.

Riparian — The area where a creek or river meets the land.

Rookery — A community of birds that live and nest in trees such as the great blue heron.

Snag — A dead tree or stump where birds (woodpeckers) bore out a hole for nesting.

Tattoo — Another term used for the drumming activity of woodpeckers on objects such as houses or dead trees. This is done to establish territory or to communicate with a mate.

Transition Zone — An area where two or more habitats touch and combine (e.g., fields and treeline).

Tripod — A three-legged devise used as a base for holding a camera, binocular or video equipment. It creates a steady platform.

WMA — Wildlife Management Area

Woodies — A common expression used for wood ducks.

Index — Land Routes

Index — Water Routes

Index — Handicapped Accessible Places

These areas have some handicapped accessible area within their boundaries or are routes you can enjoy from a car:

Index — Routes by Level of Difficulty

Word Index

E

F

G

H

I

J

K

L

M

Author Biography

Norman E. Wolfe has been a bird lover most of his life and has taken an active role in bird education and nature projects. He was a scout leader for over 20 years where he enjoyed introducing boys to the wonders of nature and birds in particular. He took his scouts on many canoe camping trips throughout the northeast and Canada.

He built many bird trails, including bluebird trails, in upstate New York where he resides.

Mr. Wolfe is a member of Cornell Lab of Ornithology, the National Audubon Society, and supports Ducks Unlimited. He works with local country clubs as a habitat, bird, and nature consultant to establish their certification in the Audubon Cooperative Sanctuary Program for Golf Courses.

In addition to birding, Mr. Wolfe enjoys nature photography and many other outdoor activities. He is a musician who has been known to carry his guitar outdoors (the piano is too heavy) and share his music in natural settings.

Other Books Available From Footprint Press

Take a Hike! Family Walks in the Rochester (NY) Area
> ISBN# 0-9656974-79   U.S. $16.95
> A guide to 60 trails for day hikes in Monroe County. Each trail has a map, description, and details such as where to park, estimated hiking time, and interesting points along the way.

Take Your Bike! Family Rides in the Rochester (NY) Area
> ISBN# 0-9656974-28   U.S. $16.95
> Converted railroad beds, paved bike paths, woods trails, and little used country roads combine to create the 30 safe bicycle adventures within an easy drive of Rochester, N.Y.

Take A Hike! Family Walks in the Finger Lakes & Genesee Valley Region (NY)
> ISBN# 0-9656974-95   U.S. $16.95
> Perfect for an afternoon walk on 51 trails through forests, glens, and bogs of upstate N.Y. Each trail has a map, description, and details such as where to park, estimated hiking time, and interesting points along the way.

Take Your Bike! Family Rides in the Finger Lakes & Genesee Valley Region (NY)
> ISBN# 0-9656974-44   U.S. $16.95
> Converted railroad beds, paved bike paths, woods trails, and little used country roads combine to create the 40 safe bicycle adventures through central and western N.Y.

Snow Trails - Cross-country Ski and Snowshoe in Central and Western New York
> ISBN# 0-9656974-52   U.S. $16.95
> Maps and descriptions of 78 trail networks to explore when our world is blanketed in white.

Bruce Trail – An Adventure Along the Niagara Escarpment
> ISBN# 0-9656974-36   U.S. $16.95
> A travel narrative of a five-week hike along the Niagara Escarpment in Ontario, Canada. Explore the now abandoned Welland Canal routes, caves formed by crashing waves, ancient cedar forests, and white cobblestone beaches along azure Georgian Bay. Learn the secrets of long-distance backpackers.

Peak Experiences – Hiking the Highest Summits of New York, County by County
> ISBN# 0-9656974-01   U.S. $16.95
> Bag the highest point in each of the 62 counties of New York State with this guidebook. Some are barely molehills that can be driven by, others are significant mountain peaks that require a full-day climb. All promise new discoveries.

Backpacking Trails of Central and Western NY   U.S. $2.00
> A 10-page booklet describing the backpackable trails of central and western New York State with contact information for obtaining maps and trail guides.

For sample maps and chapters explore web site:
http://www.footprintpress.com

Yes, I'd like to order Footprint Press books:

#

____ *Birding in Central and Western New York*	$16.95
____ *Snow Trails - Cross-country Ski in Central & Western NY*	$16.95
____ *Peak Experiences - Hiking the Summits of NY Counties*	$16.95
____ *Take A Hike! Family Walks in the Rochester (NY) Area*	$16.95
____ *Take A Hike! Family Walks in the Finger Lakes (NY)*	$16.95
____ *Take Your Bike! Family Rides in the Rochester (NY) Area*	$16.95
____ *Take Your Bike! Family Rides in the Finger Lakes (NY)*	$16.95
____ *Bruce Trail - Adventure Along the Niagara Escarpment (Canada)*	$16.95
____ *Backpacking Trails of Central & Western NY*	$2.00
____ *Alter – A Simple Path to Emotional Wellness*	$16.95

Sub-total $_____

NYS and Canadian residents add 8% tax $_____

Shipping is FREE $ FREE

Total enclosed: $_____

Your Name: _____

Address: _____

City: _____ State (Province): _____

Zip (Postal Code): _____ Country: _____

Make check payable and mail to:
Footprint Press
P.O. Box 645
Fishers, N.Y. 14453

Or, check the web site at http://www.footprintpress.com
Or, call 1-800-431-1579

Footprint Press books are available at special discounts
when purchased in bulk for sales promotions,
premiums, or fund raising.
Call (716) 421-9383 for details.